PUGET SOUND WHALES
FOR SALE

D1564409

PUGET SOUND WHALES
FOR SALE

THE FIGHT TO END ORCA HUNTING

SANDRA POLLARD

Charleston   London

THE
History
PRESS

Published by The History Press
Charleston, SC 29403
www.historypress.net

Copyright © 2014 by Sandra Pollard
All rights reserved

Back cover, inset: Southern Resident orca passing Turn Point Lighthouse, Stuart Island,
Washington. *Author collection.*
All other cover photos courtesy David Ellifrit, Center for Whale Research.

First published 2014

Manufactured in the United States

ISBN 978.1.62619.602.5

Library of Congress CIP data applied for.

For the whales

CONTENTS

FOREWORD

The infamous orca captures of the 1960s and 1970s in Washington State and British Columbia ripped dozens of whales away from their natural lives in the sea and also deeply impacted many humans. From those who watched in wonder as Namu was pulled in a makeshift pen into Puget Sound to all who saw Shamu perform routines, there are many memories and stories from those early days of orcas in bondage. Sandra Pollard's book gives us a full picture of the events, actions and key individuals from that era, still vividly recalled by many. The unique personalities of the orcas themselves are shown as they respond to brutal capture operations, clumsy transportation attempts and monotonous circus acts in sterile tanks.

By intertwining a range of perspectives on the capture operations and their aftermath, *Puget Sound Whales for Sale* provides a complete history of the short-lived but gut-wrenching exploitation of Salish Sea orcas. Now, decades later, we understand orcas a little better. Field studies begun following the captures have shown that orcas live as loyal family members, bonded to one another in ancient traditional cultures, communicating in ways beyond the reach of modern science, always in harmony with their kin. While being pursued, orcas acted as decoys to confuse the capture teams yet never harmed any human during the violent capture operations. Even when mothers were driven away from their netted calves, they refrained from attacking their captors. That mystery and many more are illuminated in these pages.

—Howard Garrett

PREFACE

I t's a story that could best be told in a book." Those were the words used by Wallie Funk under the title *The Great Penn Cove Whale Catch, 1970*, one of the noteworthy events featured in the Christmas postcard he and his wife, Mary Ann, sent out to family and friends in December 1994. I knew nothing about that statement when, in 2010, an essay I wrote titled "Whale Watching" was one of the winning entries in the Northwest Institute of Literary Arts Spirit of Writing Contest, which is sponsored by the Whidbey Island Writers Association. The essay told the story of the notorious 1970 Penn Cove capture in Washington State and piqued the interest of a fellow writer, who asked what I intended to do with the material. It was a question I was already asking myself. A 1,200-word essay cannot encompass the finer details of a decade of changing attitudes, politics and legislation, and many pertinent questions about the orca capture era in Washington State remained unanswered.

An initial quest for information revealed fragmented articles and stories, but there was little continuity. I set out to fit the pieces of the jigsaw together and to interweave the chain of events leading up to the final brutal capture of six Transient killer whales in Budd Inlet, Olympia, in 1976. I also set out to discover what had happened to all those whales bought and sold for marine parks to satisfy the public's insatiable desire for "entertainment."

This is the story of the charismatic Southern Resident killer whales, a distinct population of a specific ecotype that inhabits the Salish Sea, a body of water located in the northwest corner of Washington State and southern British Columbia. In November 2005, the National Marine Fisheries Service (NMFS), founded in 1871 as the U.S. Commission on Fish and Fisheries, listed the Southern Residents as "endangered" under the 1973 Endangered Species Act. Their journey to this protected status was a protracted one, involving the capture and killing of approximately one-third to one-half of their population. It was a high price to pay, fueled not only by man's desire for domination and power but also personal and corporate greed. These factors, among others, have contributed to the decimation of a small population of whales, from which they are still struggling to recover many years later.

Whale watching in the United States is now a multimillion-dollar industry, with the ocean's top predator drawing the crowds—but not only in the wild. Killer whales are popular tourist attractions at marine parks throughout the world, where they routinely perform a cycle of tricks and stunts daily. Many of those whales are captive-born, but that has not always been the case. There are those who have known the wild, who learned how to hunt for their food and recognized the unique dialect calls of other members of their pod. Many of the Southern Residents came into that category, including Lolita, the only surviving Southern Resident from the capture era still in captivity.

The aim of this book is to serve not only as a reminder about the precious gift we almost lost but also as a tribute and memorial to those whales whose lives were stolen from them. Let us not forget, either, their cousins the Northern Residents in Canada and all the other whales torn from their families during more than a decade of violent captures. Lastly, let us not forget those whales in captivity today that have never known the open ocean or the strong bonds holding their cohesive family units together or, most of all, the joy of freedom.

ACKNOWLEDGEMENTS

A lthough a book is usually written by one person, many other people contribute toward it, whether it be a work of fiction or nonfiction. This book is no exception. My husband, Richard, has provided constant support and encouragement throughout the lengthy research and writing process, as have my mother, Doreen; my son, Jeremy; and his wife, Katarina. I am indebted to Howard Garrett and Susan Berta of Orca Network, the nonprofit Whidbey Island–based whale education and sightings organization, for their invaluable help and faith in my credibility as a writer to do justice to the story of the Southern Resident killer whales.

I would also like to thank those people who agreed to talk about their personal experiences of the orca capture era (1965–1976) in Washington State, including former longtime secretary of state Ralph Munro (1980–2001) and Karen Hanson Munro. Marine mammal biologist Dr. Terrell Newby, who was present at the 1970 Penn Cove capture on Whidbey Island, willingly gave his time to provide insight into the perception of killer whale captures at that time. Wallie V. Funk, former co-owner and editor of the *Anacortes American*, *South Whidbey Record* and *Whidbey News-Times*, brought the 1970 Penn Cove capture story alive through his journalistic and photographic skills. Western Washington University's State Archive Department houses many of Wallie Funk's photographs and proved an important source of reference, along with the *Whidbey News-Times*'s archived newspaper reports.

Historian Dave Hastings (now retired) located and prepared files at the state archives office in Olympia, which provided a wealth of material.

ACKNOWLEDGEMENTS

Once again, thank you to Ralph Munro for ensuring that newspaper cuttings and documents recording the events of that time were retained for future reference.

Orca: The Whale Called Killer by Erich Hoyt has been a significant research tool and provided much of the basis for tracing the fates of the many whales captured. My thanks to the author not only for writing a finely crafted book but also for the diligent work undertaken in collating statistics and information. It was a pleasure to meet Erich Hoyt in person at the World Whale Conference, WhaleFest 2012, in Brighton, UK.

Many people have contributed with their stories, newspaper articles, photographs and information. They include first and foremost Howard Garrett and Susan Berta; researchers Kenneth C. Balcomb III, David Ellifrit and Stefan Jacobs, Center for Whale Research, San Juan Island; Graeme Ellis, Pacific Biological Station; Dr. Michael Ford, Northwest Fisheries Science Center; Dr. Ingrid N. Visser, Orca Research Trust; Dr. Naomi A. Rose, Humane Society of the United States; veterinarian Dr. Pete Schroeder, who accompanied the original Shamu to SeaWorld San Diego; Captain John Colby Stone, Pixie Maylor, Lyla Snover and Joe Beckley (1970 Penn Cove capture); Connie Bickerton and Joan Bickerton (newspaper cuttings and photos of "Whale"); Mimi Sheridan, who kindly shared the late Don McGaffin's personal account of the 1971 Penn Cove capture; Doug Cartlidge (former trainer); investigative journalist Tim Zimmerman, who was generous enough to share a rare interview with Donald Goldsberry, one of the two men responsible for carrying out many of the captures; Stefan Freelan, cartographer; Uko Gorter, natural history illustrator; and Kelli Clifton, artist.

Thank you to author David Kirby for editorial guidance in polishing the manuscript, to copy editor Audrey Mackaman and to literary agent Andrea Hurst, who gave her time and advice freely through the medium of Whidbey Island writers' group, Just Write.

Credit must go to commissioning editor Will McKay of The History Press for the efficient, patient and cheerful manner in which he dealt with my questions; to project editor Darcy Mahan; and to all other members of the staff who worked to put this book together. I am most grateful to Whidbey Island author Elizabeth Guss for her introduction to The History Press.

My heartfelt thanks to each and every one for their help in bringing an important slice of Washington State history to life, and my sincere apologies to anyone whose name I have inadvertently omitted.

What is a man without the beasts?
If all the beasts were gone, man would die from a great loneliness of spirit.
For whatever happens to the beast soon happens to the man.
All things are connected.
—attributed to Chief Seattle

CHAPTER 1

THE LEGEND AND THE MONSTER

Puget Sound, Washington State, which forms part of the Salish Sea, is made up of a myriad of interconnecting channels and waterways, partly estuarine and partly marine. The term "Salish Sea" was first used in 1988 by Bert Webber, a marine biologist from Bellingham, Washington, and officially adopted in 2009 to honor the Coast Salish people and describe the waters of the Strait of Georgia, the Strait of Juan de Fuca and Puget Sound.[1] The Salish Sea also encompasses the adjoining waters of Bellingham Bay, Rosario Strait and Haro Strait, as well as the waters around the San Juan Islands, Washington, and the Southern Gulf Islands, British Columbia.

The definition of a sound in relation to a body of water is an inlet, bay or narrow area of water between an island and the mainland.[2] Admiralty Inlet, lying between the northeastern part of the Olympic Peninsula and Whidbey Island, is the major connection feeding into the Strait of Juan de Fuca and the Pacific Ocean. Generally considered to be Puget Sound's main basin, Admiralty Inlet's northern boundary runs between Point Wilson and Point Partridge, extending south to the southern tip of Whidbey Island and Point No Point, located on the Kitsap Peninsula. The area stretches 169.0 square miles and is 3.7 miles wide at the narrowest point between the lighthouses at Point Wilson and Admiralty Head. First discovered in 1790 by Manuel Quimper's Spanish expedition, Admiralty Inlet was named Ensenada de Caamaño after naval officer Jacinto Caamaño. Two years later, Ensenada de Caamaño was renamed Admiralty Inlet when the British explorer Captain George Vancouver arrived on the scene.

Map of the Salish Sea. *Courtesy Stefan Freelan, Western Washington University.*

Deception Pass, a fast-flowing strait with whirlpools and strong currents at the north end of Whidbey Island, is the minor connection. Like Admiralty Inlet, it was first discovered by Quimper's expedition before being mapped by Joseph Whidbey, a member of Captain George Vancouver's 1792 expedition. An initial exploration of the waters on the east side of Whidbey Island fooled the seafarers, who after exploring Saratoga Passage turned back from the shallow waters of Skagit Bay, missing the pass. It was not until they sailed north along the west side of Whidbey Island and came across the rock-lined narrow channel that they realized they had been "deceived" and Whidbey was, in fact, an island. Since July 1935, Whidbey Island has been connected at the north end to mainland Fidalgo Island by Deception Pass Bridge.[3]

Puget Sound, which extends approximately one hundred miles from Deception Pass to Olympia, was named after Lieutenant Peter Puget, another member of Captain Vancouver's 1792 expedition. In the hope that Admiralty Inlet and Georgia Strait might lead to the Northwest Passage, Captain Vancouver anchored HMS *Discovery* near Seattle (named after the Duwamish chief Seattle), while Lieutenant Puget took charge of a small expedition to explore the area. Captain Vancouver claimed Puget Sound (south of Tacoma Narrows) for Great Britain on June 4, 1792. Later, Puget Sound encompassed the waters north of Tacoma Narrows.

Deception Pass Bridge spanning Whidbey and Fidalgo Islands. *Author collection.*

Two snowcapped mountain ranges, the Cascades and the Olympics, border Puget Sound on either side, providing seasonal fresh water. A number of salmon-bearing rivers feed into the sound, including the Nooksack, which flows into Bellingham Bay, and the Elwha and Dungeness, which flow into the Strait of Juan de Fuca. The Chilliwack River flows north to the Fraser River in Canada.

It is in the relatively protected inland waters of the Salish Sea that the endangered Southern Resident killer whales spend much of their time during the summer months in search of Chinook, or "King" salmon. Chinook is the largest species of salmon native to the Pacific Northwest and constitutes 80 percent of the Southern Residents' diet. Like the whales, some runs of Chinook salmon are endangered.

Chief Seattle, 1864. *Museum of History and Industry, Seattle.*

It is also in these seemingly calm and pristine waters that the Southern Residents lost one-third to one-half of their population during Washington State's capture era. In 2005, the same year that the Southern Resident killer whales were listed as endangered, the orca was adopted as the official marine mammal of Washington State, an iconic symbol intended to promote species awareness and encourage protection of the natural marine habitat.

So why, when the orca is now enjoying protected and almost film star status, were they persecuted for so long? To create an understanding of the shift in attitude, it is necessary to look back in time at the history of man's changing relationship with the ocean's top predator.

As far back as 100 BC, records exist in Peru of temples dedicated to killer whales and paintings depicting killer whales as symbols of courage, fertility and power. Even in those early days, these mysterious and mythical creatures of the deep were feared. In AD 50, the Roman naturalist and writer Pliny the Elder witnessed a stranded killer whale being publicly slaughtered in Ostia

THE FIGHT TO END ORCA HUNTING

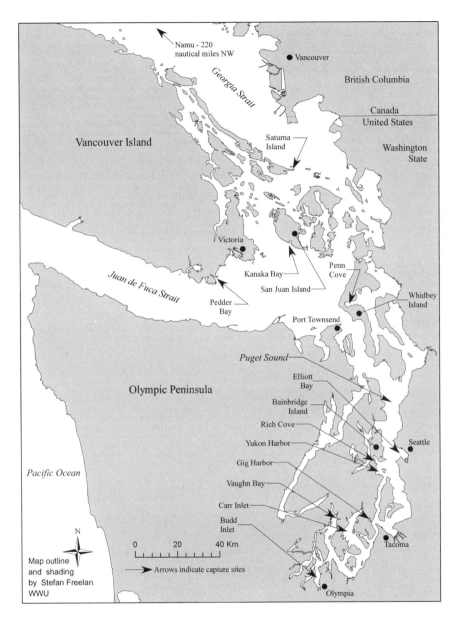

Map showing capture site locations (as marked by Richard Snowberger). *Map image courtesy Stefan Freelan, Western Washington University.*

Harbor, Rome. The killer whale's reputation as a fierce, savage monster that would kill not only other whales and dolphins but also humans was predominant for many centuries.

In 1758, Carolus Linnaeus, a Swedish botanist, designated the name "*Orcinus orca*" (*Orcinus* meaning "of or belonging to the realms of the dead," *orca* meaning "a kind of whale") for the killer whale. *Orcinus orca* is, in fact, the largest member of the dolphin family and a member of the suborder of *Odontoceti*, or toothed whale. Like other marine mammals that made the transition from land to sea, they are warmblooded, breathe air through their lungs, give birth to live young and, at some time in their lives, have hair.

Orcas, which vary in size and color across the planet, can grow up to thirty-two feet in length, with an adult male (referred to as a "bull") weighing up to approximately twenty-two thousand pounds.[4] Males in the wild can live from fifty to sixty-plus years (the average age is twenty-nine) with the onset of sexual maturity at twelve to fifteen years of age. Physical maturity is a little later, at age twenty, when the "sprouting" dorsal fin reaches its full height of up to six feet.

Females (referred to as "cows") are smaller, growing up to twenty-eight feet and weighing up to 16,500 pounds. In the wild, females can live from ninety to more than one hundred years (the average age is fifty) and are reproductive from about eleven to forty-five years of age (although in captivity females as young as seven years old have borne young), and give birth to a single calf on average every three to five years. There is no specific mating time. Breeding takes place between the pods, and most calves are born in the winter after a seventeen- or eighteen-month gestation period.

Calves (a year to a year and a half) are seven to eight feet long when born and weigh three hundred to four hundred pounds. The young swim in their mother's slipstream, the area of least resistance, and nurse for at least a year. Survival rate of the firstborn is only 40 percent due to the presence of toxins, such as polychlorinated biphenyls (PCBs) and polybrominated biphenyl ethers (PBDEs), which are offloaded in the mother's milk. Siblings born subsequently stand a better chance of survival.

Whales aged between a year and a half to ten years are termed juveniles, while those between ten and sixteen to seventeen are termed adolescents. From then on, the whales are referred to as adults.

The Southern Resident fish-eating population, one of three ecotypes of killer whale that inhabit the Salish Sea (the other two are the mammal-eating Transients, also known as Bigg's killer whales, and the rarely seen shark-eaters known as the Offshores), is made up of three pods: J, K and L.

KILLER WHALES
Northern Hemisphere
ecotypes & forms

Resident Killer Whale

Bigg's Killer Whale
(transient)

Offshore Killer Whale

Type 1 Eastern North Atlantic

Type 2 Eastern North Atlantic

0   meters   10

Orcinus Orca, Killer Whales, Ecotypes & Forms. Illustration by and courtesy of Uko Gorter.

Since 1976, when biologist Ken Balcomb of the Center for Whale Research on San Juan Island began his studies, their numbers have fluctuated between seventy-one in 1976 and ninety-eight in 1995, the highest number recorded. L pod is the largest of the three, followed by J pod and K pod. Physically, they are a little smaller than other killer whales, the males reaching twenty-one to

Members of L pod cruising the Salish Sea. *David Ellifrit, Center for Whale Research.*

twenty-three feet in length and the females reaching eighteen to twenty-one feet in length; these measurements remain in accord with the average for killer whales across the world.[5] The three pods, known as a clan, have their own distinct culture, diet, social structure and vocalizations. Each pod has a specific dialect of around twelve different calls, while the three pods share around thirty calls between them.

Using their highly evolved sense of echolocation, the Southern Resident orcas hunt and forage in search of their traditional choice of food, the favored Chinook salmon. Rich in calories and omega-3 fats, the highly prized Chinook provides much-needed energy and "brain food." With their forty to fifty-two interlocking conical teeth, each whale consumes an average of 145 pounds of Chinook salmon daily (a fully grown salmon measures thirty-three to thirty-six inches long and weighs 40 to 50 pounds).

The Southern Residents' range is quite extensive. During the summer months, they spend much of their time around the archipelago of the richly forested and reefed San Juan Islands, a Mecca for boaters, tourists and whale-watchers alike. In the fall, they venture into the inland waterways of Puget Sound in search of Chum salmon, their second-favorite choice of food. Over the winter months, they have been observed as far south as Monterey, California, and as far north as southeast Alaska. With their ability to cover up to one hundred miles a day and with a swimming capacity of up to thirty miles per hour, they are able to traverse the waters of the Pacific Northwest at will, although all three pods may not travel together at the same time.

With eyesight as sharp above water as below, killer whales are often seen raising their heads and the top part of their body above the surface to look around, an activity known as "spy-hopping." Other behaviors include breaching, when the full body arcs through the air, tail lobbing (smacking flukes on the surface of the water), lunging (after food), rolling, "porpoising" (propelling themselves forward, upward and out of the water) and slapping the water with their pectoral fins. A behavior believed to be unique to the Southern Residents is the ritualized "greeting ceremony," when all three pods group up and exhibit aerial dynamics and rapid milling action.

Resident orcas live in pods, or family groups, which stay together for life. There is no dispersal. The social structure is matrilineal, whereby ancestry is traced through the female and is made up of an older female (referred to as a matriarch), her offspring and their offspring. Sons stay with their mothers, while daughters may branch off and create their own matriline. Even so, the family remains a close-knit unit, with older members sharing the care of the young.

Deadhead (K27) spy-hopping with son Ripple (K44) surfacing nearby. *David Ellifrit, Center for Whale Research.*

Lea (K14) breaching in front of Center for Whale Research, San Juan Island. *David Ellifrit, Center for Whale Research.*

Matia (L77) and daughter Joy (L119) swimming in her mother's slipstream. *David Ellifrit, Center for Whale Research.*

 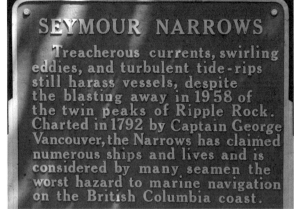

Above, left: Native American art sculpture of eagle and killer whale by E. Williams, Duncan, Vancouver Island, British Columbia. *Author collection.*

Above, right: Plaque at Seymour Narrows Lookout, Campbell River, Vancouver Island, British Columbia, to mark the blasting of Ripple Rock. *Author collection.*

In Native American society, killer whales play an important part in the culture of the indigenous people of the Pacific Northwest. Revered as creatures of myth and legend, their iconic status is displayed in art and sculpture and is predominant in bold, colorful tribal crests. Symbolically, the whale represents intelligence, compassion, unity and goodness.

Perceived as the most powerful animals in the ocean, custodians of the seas and rulers of the undersea world, orcas are believed to embody the souls of chiefs. This factor was instrumental in preventing the capture of Luna (L98), a Southern Resident juvenile male born in September 1999 that became separated from his pod and strayed into Nootka Sound, British Columbia, in 2001.

But as European influence grew, other attitudes to the killer whale developed. Like a chameleon changing color, the creature of myth and legend took on the mantle of a terrifying, cold-blooded monster bent on the death and destruction of everything in its path, including humans. Fishermen, who hated and feared the voracious predator they blamed for devouring the salmon they wanted for themselves, attributed the name "blackfish" to this dangerous, ravenous thief. In the 1960s, the U.S. military used the vicious, man-eating killers as target practice on strafing runs. A machine gun was set up overlooking Seymour Narrows, a dangerous body of water between Discovery Passage and Johnstone Strait at the southern end of Vancouver Island, British Columbia, to shoot at marauding whales heading toward Campbell River, one of Vancouver Island's prime fishing areas. The gun was never used, but the intent was there. Even so, 25 percent of killer whales captured for aquariums and marine parks during the 1960s and 1970s were found to have bullet wounds in their blubber.

The prospect of hunting and capturing these fearsome creatures on the open seas may have been entertained by hard-bitten trophy hunters but just as readily dismissed. Accidental catch was one thing. Setting out to wrestle and contain a mighty killer whale with the itinerant risk of injury or death was another. But since time immemorial, man has been unable to resist the hunt and thrill of the chase, driven by dreams of glory and the prospect of food or riches. It was only a matter of time before someone would try his hand at taking or killing the monster from the deep. If and when they succeeded, the future of the Southern Residents, along with that of other killer whales, would be in jeopardy forever.

CHAPTER 2
MOBY DOLL

One of the first people known to attempt to capture a live killer whale was Frank Brocato, head of animal collections for Marineland of the Pacific. The marine park, located south of Los Angeles, operated from 1954 until 1987 before being bought out and subsequently closed by SeaWorld of San Diego. In November 1961, Brocato and his assistant, Frank "Boots" Calandrino, captured a female killer whale that had strayed into the harbor at Newport Beach, California. Watched by an estimated eight thousand people, "six determined men struggled six hours yesterday before capturing a two-ton killer whale, possibly the first of its kind ever taken alive. The whale was caught in a net, loaded onto a truck, and hauled off to a new home at Marineland."[1]

Wanda, as the whale was christened, did not survive. She was probably ailing when she found her way into the harbor. After being transferred to a one-hundred-foot,[2] three-story-high, 540,000-gallon tank containing three thousand fish,[3] seventeen-foot-long Wanda smashed her head repeatedly against the walls and died three days after being captured. The results of the autopsy on Wanda revealed "gastroenteritis and pneumonia."[4]

Despite Wanda's demise and emboldened by their earlier success, Brocato and Calandrino took their forty-foot boat *Geronimo*[5] and ventured into Puget Sound in the late summer of the following year to look for another killer whale. After searching for a month for the telltale sight of dorsal fins and blows among the myriad of islands and waterways, they discovered a mature male and a female in Haro Strait, near San Juan Island. The female, a mammal-eating Transient intent on chasing a porpoise in her sights, cut across the bow of the boat in hot pursuit of the fleeing animal. Seizing their opportunity, Brocato and Calandrino, like a couple of cowboys roping cattle, lassoed the whale before she dove. As she turned, the lasso's nylon line caught around the boat's propeller shaft, bringing the vessel to an abrupt, shuddering halt. Taking up the full 250-foot line, the female surfaced emitting high-pitched, piercing cries. When the male rejoined her, the pair, fighting for their survival, charged toward the boat several times, hitting it with the full force of their massive flukes.

Brocato reached for his .375-magnum rifle and shot one bullet into the male, who disappeared. The female was not so lucky. Brocato peppered her thick blubber with another ten shots, maiming and finally killing her. The triumphant hunter towed his slain quarry's bloody, bullet-ridden carcass back to Bellingham for delivery to a rendering plant, to be ignominiously turned into dog food. To ensure that his prized acquisition did not become merely a distant memory, the conquering hero reputedly kept the whale's three-inch-long, conical teeth as a trophy.

These are the first known instances of attempts to capture killer whales using, in the second instance, the lasso or hoop netting method. An article by George W. Klontz, M.S., D.V.M., titled "Medical Care of Newly Captured Killer Whales" pertaining to the capture of whales in Puget Sound, Washington State, in 1967 and 1968, explains how the technique worked.[6]

As soon as the whale was caught, a nylon noose was placed behind the pectoral fins with a breakaway hoop. An alternative capture method was to drop a net over the whale, entangling it. Both options carried the risk of drowning or causing the whale to inhale enough water to contribute to pneumonia.

Once the whale was restrained alongside a skiff, a "bag net" of nylon mesh was placed over the head. This was secured behind the dorsal fin and the net drawn tight, creating a "bridle." The net was cut to enable the pectoral fins to be extended and thus allow the whale to swim while still being controlled by its captors. Although later the more "humane" seine netting capture method came into operation, hoop netting was still used to separate and secure the whales.

But let's not forget the harpoon…

In 1964, the Vancouver Public Aquarium, British Columbia, under the direction of curator Dr. Murray Newman, hired local sculptor Samuel Burich, who was selected by the principal of the School of Art, to find and kill a killer whale. The plan was to kill the whale and take underwater photographs so that the body shape could be studied and copied to a life-sized model for use as an exhibit. Newman wanted to have the finest aquarium in the world, complete with the best exhibit—a killer whale.

In May of that year, Burich set up a three-foot-long steel harpoon gun acquired from Coal Harbor, British Columbia, on the east side of Saturna Island, one of the Southern Gulf Islands midway between Vancouver Island and the lower mainland of British Columbia. In mid-July, as he and his fellow hunters were about to pack up camp after an unrequited two-and-a-half-month vigil, Burich sighted a dozen or so killer whales shortly before midday. Carefully maneuvering the lethal weapon and aiming it in the direction of a young fifteen-foot killer whale, Burich pulled the gun's trigger. His aim went true. The sharply pointed steel harpoon shaft hit the whale in the fatty tissue behind the skull, piercing the intricate framework of nerves and muscle and disorienting but not killing the juvenile mammal. When speaking about his victory to the *Vancouver Sun*, Burich told the reporter, "I picked out one that seemed a little smaller than the others. It looked me right in the eye and I looked right back. I just let her have it."[7]

It is a known behavior that whales and dolphins will support an ailing member of the pod at the surface to help them breathe. In accord with their close-knit family unity, other members of the pod remained with the stricken whale, pushing and nudging the animal toward the surface before eventually swimming away. Once alone, the wounded creature made a valiant effort to free herself of the impaled harpoon. Emitting shrill, high-pitched whistles, the whale twisted repeatedly, violently thrashing her tail flukes in a doomed attempt to escape from the searing agony inflicted by the metal shaft.

By early afternoon, the whale, with at least two extra bullets lodged in her blubber, was still fighting hard for its life. Burich and a professional fisherman, Joe Bauer, tried to wrangle the struggling, bloodied animal from their forty-foot fishing boat, *Corsair*.[8] To prevent islanders from shooting more bullets into the whale, Bauer pulled himself out on a rope between the flailing animal and the rifles.

On arrival at the turbulent scene, Newman decided in the interests of science that it would be better to try to keep the injured whale alive. Using the harpoon line attached to the base of the whale's dorsal fin, the weakened victim was dragged along on a twelve-hour overnight journey through rough seas, heavy rain and wind-driven squalls to a makeshift pen in Burrard dry docks, Vancouver.[9] Among the eager reception committee of scientists and biologists awaiting the whale's arrival was Dr. Pat McGeer, a liberal legislator and University of British Columbia researcher, who sought to test the whale's heartbeat using an electrocardiogram. Representatives from Woods Hole Oceanographic Institute, Massachusetts, stood by to record and study sounds and vocalizations.[10]

Waiting to greet the whale were not only a mixed bunch of researchers and scientists but also a number of angry animal rights representatives. Members of the Society for the Prevention of Cruelty to Animals accused the hunters of causing unnecessary suffering, describing the aquarium-based project as "crazy." That was not the opinion shared by North American scientists, according to Newman. He informed the press that many of them had telephoned and sent telegrams congratulating him on the capture. Soon the whale had a price on its head, including an offer of $20,000 from Marineland of the Pacific, Los Angeles.[11] Newman was not interested and turned down all offers.

For the first time ever, a killer whale became the recipient of antibiotics. The dosage, estimated at being twice that required for a horse, was administered by shooting the drug into the animal from a basket suspended from a one-hundred-foot derrick.[12]

Moby Doll circles the pen as curious bystanders watch. *Courtesy of* Vancouver Sun.

Three days after being harpooned and pumped full of penicillin to heal the festering wound, the whale was considered well enough to receive visitors. Although doubts had been raised about the whale's sex, the assistant curator of the aquarium, Vince Penfold, believed there was a "slightly better than 50 per cent" chance the animal was female.[13] By now the whale had been nicknamed "Hound Dog" because of her docile temperament, but before long the name was replaced by "Moby Doll," which had been chosen from a popular radio contest.

Despite the antibiotics, Moby Doll refused to eat. Not only were the scientists concerned about her lack of appetite, they wondered if she might be pregnant. Nobody could understand the strange noises and squeals she made, but all were relieved and delighted when she ate a couple of ten-pound salmon. She was also given vitamin B12 injections administered in four separate darts, two of which bounced off her resilient frame.

Moby Doll was not destined to stay long at the dry dock. As soon as the tides were favorable, Newman arranged for her to be moved to a pen at Jericho Beach, an abandoned Canadian navy base. Moby Doll did not adapt well to her new home, swimming endlessly in counterclockwise circles in her quest for escape and the open ocean. She showed no interest in food despite being offered such diverse temptations as horses' hearts and live octopus.[14]

Addressing the press, Newman said he suspected Moby Doll might be getting nourishment by swallowing some of the sea life in her pen. He told reporters that sperm whales, the largest of the toothed whales, obtained nourishment that way, but the "smaller, vicious killer whales live mainly on a diet of meat."

Eventually, at a loss to persuade Moby Doll to eat, Newman telephoned Marineland of the Pacific for advice. When told that smaller whales at Marineland had their mouths forced open and fish tossed in with tongs, he announced that he would not be trying that tactic on Moby Doll with her "big mouthful of flesh-tearing teeth."

On the fifty-fifth day of her captivity, Moby Doll broke her fast, but it was too late. Despite consuming up to two hundred pounds of fish daily, she was found dead at the bottom of the pen on October 9, 1964.[15]

Moby Doll remains a legend. She was the first-known captive killer whale, attracting thousands of visitors, including the Duke and Duchess of Windsor from Great Britain, who marveled at her gentleness and docility.[16] Another less well-known visitor who came to see the Vancouver Aquarium's prized exhibit was a young man from Seattle, Ted Griffin, a secret observer with an agenda of his own.

For Samuel Burich, his commission to capture and kill a whale proved a life-changing experience. He spent his spare time at Moby Doll's pen whistling and playing tunes on his mouth organ to the attentive listener, deprived of the company of her own kind. Burich could see that the strikingly marked black-and-white fish-eating marine mammal he had hunted down was a far cry from the image of the mindless man-eating plunderer hellbent on the death and destruction of everything in its path.

When a necropsy was conducted on Moby Doll, it was discovered that "she" was an adolescent male. Exhaustion and subsequent drowning and/or a skin disease occasioned by the harbor water's low salinity were found to be the cause of Moby Doll's sad demise. His death, reported in the *Times* of London, one of Britain's top tabloids, carried a two-column obituary.[17] For the first time in history, killer whales received some positive press.

Moby Doll also made history of another, darker kind. Although the fact was not known at the time, years later, the vocalizations recorded during his short life in captivity were found to belong to the Southern Resident community. He was the first Southern Resident (a member of J pod) to be captured—but by no means the last.

CHAPTER 3

A MAN ON A MISSION

There are two names synonymous with the capturing of killer whales in the Pacific Northwest. One is Donald Goldsberry, and the other is Edward "Ted" Irving Griffin. Both men plied their trade on the waters of Washington State and British Columbia during the 1960s and 1970s.

Born in 1935, Ted Griffin's fascination with the mysteries of the underwater world started at an early age. From his exploratory forays among the rich and colorful sea life of Puget Sound, home of the six-gilled shark and giant Pacific octopus, sprang an enduring vision—he wanted Seattle to have its own Marineland.

With the advent of Seattle World's Fair in June 1962, Griffin's wish became reality. He opened Seattle's first public aquarium along the waterfront at Pier 56, following in the footsteps of the entrepreneurial Ivar Haglund of Ivar's Fish Bar. Ivar's aquarium on Pier 54 opened in 1938 and closed in 1956, although his famous fish restaurant remains a popular venue for locals and tourists alike.

From the start, Griffin aimed high. Not content with housing a few select specimens of fish at the aquarium, he acquired some dolphins from another exhibit set up for the fair's opening. Since childhood, when he had seen a picture of a boy riding on a dolphin's back, he had been intrigued by the beauty and intelligence of the agile, graceful creatures. Now a young man in his twenties with drive and ambition, he dreamed of one day swimming with the largest member of the dolphin family—the killer whale.[1]

Donald C. Goldsberry. *Wallie V. Funk Photographs, Center for Pacific Northwest Studies, Western Libraries Heritage Resources, Western Washington University–Bellingham.*

Three years after starting up the aquarium and inspired by his visit to Moby Doll, Griffin's wild dream came true. In June 1965, fisherman Bill Lechkobit was caught in a gale off Warrior Cove, just south of the small coastal fishing village of Namu, British Columbia, which lies about seventy miles north of Port Hardy, Vancouver Island. To avoid his boat being dragged onto rocks, Lechkobit cut his nets loose and headed for the welcome shelter of home.[2]

The following morning, after the storm had abated, another fisherman, Bob McGarvey, discovered two killer whales, one an adult male and the other a calf, trapped inside the net. As the current swept the end of the net open, the bull swam away. When the calf did not follow, the bull returned.

Remembering how much fame and publicity Moby Doll had attracted, the two fishermen realized they had a potentially valuable asset on their hands—two, in fact. Once they had secured the netting around the whales (nicknamed "Romeo and Juliet") and believing their fortunes to be assured, Lechkobit and McGarvey announced their prized acquisition to the outside world. Murray Newman, director of the Vancouver Aquarium, was one of the prospective buyers who arrived to barter for the whales—and so was Ted Griffin, who wasted no time in getting there.

When Lechkobit and McGarvey put up an asking price of $25,000 for each whale, no deals were done. The price became even less attractive to potential buyers when it was made clear that the cost of transportation was not included. In a twist of fate, the calf managed to slip away a few days later, making good its escape, unlike the bull. The fishermen now found themselves lumbered with a nine-thousand-pound adult male complete with the dual challenges of housing and transporting such a huge animal—a far less appealing proposition to aquariums.

In a bid to rid themselves of their rather dubious possession, Lechkobit and McGarvey announced, "The first person here with $8,000 in cash gets the whale."

Above, left: Edward "Ted" Griffin. *Wallie V. Funk Photographs, Center for Pacific Northwest Studies, Western Libraries Heritage Resources, Western Washington University–Bellingham.*

Above, right: Pier 56, Trident Imports and Seattle Marine Aquarium, July 7, 1964. *Courtesy of the Seattle Public Library.*

Below: Pier 56 and Seattle Marine Aquarium, June 1962. *Courtesy of the Seattle Public Library.*

Word reached Griffin in Seattle on Saturday. Despite having already traveled to Namu and returned empty-handed, Griffin saw his once-in-a-lifetime opportunity. There was just one problem. He had no money.

Undeterred by the fact that it was a weekend and no banks were open, the energetic and enterprising Griffin set off around the Seattle waterfront the next morning calling on hotels, restaurants and local businesses to help him raise the cash. Soon he was on his way north, cash in hand.

The sale of the whale to Griffin was not popular with everyone. The two fishermen turned down the Vancouver Aquarium and Victoria Undersea Aquarium's joint offer of $3,000 in cash by way of deposit, to be followed by a further payment of $6,000 when the whale was safely in their possession. A meeting of members of the local branch of the United Fishermen and Allied Workers' Union, who were incensed at the prospect of the whale being purchased by Americans "because they have more money," sent a barrage of telegrams to provincial and federal agencies requesting assistance to help raise funds to enable the Vancouver Aquarium to buy the whale.[3]

After handing over the cash and closing the deal, Griffin's next challenge was to find a way of transporting the whale four hundred miles south to Seattle, hardly an everyday occurrence. Griffin figured out a strategy: he had steel bars welded into a sixty- by forty- by sixteen-foot three-sided pen with help from local fishermen. Empty oil drums obtained from a local salvage company kept the pen afloat, and a net was hung across its open side.[4]

Meanwhile, still trapped at Warrior Cove, the captive whale waited—but not alone. Other whales swam and circled nearby, including a female and two calves, their high-pitched vocalizations and calls resounding in the quiet, secluded inlet as they communicated with their lost relative.

Once the steel mesh cage was completed, Goldsberry, a commercial fisherman and animal collector from the Tacoma Municipal Aquarium, arrived to direct the transfer operation. The two men had become acquainted when both were attempting to capture killer whales in Puget Sound. Realizing they shared a common goal, the pair teamed up into the lethal partnership that would culminate in the capturing and killing of many whales in the waters of Washington State over the next decade.

Timing of the transfer was of the essence. Before Griffin dove to cut the nets so the whale could swim into the cage, Goldsberry warned him that he would only get one chance with the tide and prevailing currents.

Much to Griffin's relief, the whale did not make a bid for freedom and entered the pen. Two hours later, the tugboat towing the caged whale arrived at the cannery town of Namu. As the boat docked with its unusual floating cargo, legend has it that a young boy cried out, "Namu, Namu." The whale had found a name.

That was but the beginning of Namu's epic journey. On July 9, the purse-seiner *Chamiss Bay* (this fishing method, originally developed in Denmark, resembles drawing the strings of a purse together, hence the name "purse seine"—a rope passes through a number of rings along the bottom of the net which, when pulled, brings the rings close to one another, trapping the catch) took over the tow across the Inside Passage waters of Queen Charlotte Sound to Port Hardy, a fishing town located on the northeastern side of Vancouver Island, British Columbia. The *Chamiss Bay* was accompanied by the *Robert E. Lee*, a pleasure tug owned by Seattle disc jockey Bob Hardwick. Such was the media frenzy over the whale that journalists on the *Robert E. Lee* reported daily on Namu's progress, fueling and satisfying the intense public interest. Gil Hewlett, a twenty-four-year-old Canadian biologist loaned from the Vancouver Aquarium to help with the transfer, monitored the whale's respiration rate and food intake. He also endeavored to record the animal's calls.

Griffin was greeted by curious onlookers on arrival at Port Hardy two days later. There, he learned that the Canadian Fishermen's Union planned to prevent the export of Namu. A reception committee from the "Free the Whale" movement also awaited Griffin's party, with a woman giving full vent to her feelings as she screamed, "Shame on you!"[5]

After repairing damage occasioned to the pen on the stormy Queen Charlotte Sound crossing, the tow was transferred to ninety-foot Seattle-based tug *Iver Foss*. The tugboat was not far out from Port Hardy before a female orca and two calves began to follow it. Was this the same family that had kept their mournful vigil near Namu's pen in Warrior Cove? Perhaps one of the calves was the same calf for which Namu had traded his freedom. Hewlett recorded the following entry in a journal:[6]

> *When they are within 300 yards of the pen, Namu lets out a terrifying squeal, almost like a throttled cat. He leaps out of the water and crashes against the left corner of the pen. There was terrific thrashing and he is making all kinds of sounds. Then they are there again, the same family of the cow and two calves. They came straight up behind the pen to about ten feet away, tremendous squealing going on. Namu seemed to lose all co-ordination [sic] in the pen. He kept getting swept against the cargo net and swimming vigorously forward. The family unit circles around towards the end of the pen.*

As the flotilla headed toward Seymour Narrows on the northeast side of Vancouver Island, Namu's faithful companions fell behind. Years later, researchers learned that the treacherous piece of water forms the boundary between the perceived ranges of the Northern and Southern Resident communities. Passing through the narrows, described by Captain Vancouver as "one of the vilest stretches of water in the world," Namu was buffeted constantly inside his steel cage by the fierce currents and strong tidal surges.

Having survived the turbulent two-hour passage, the whale suffered further discomfort from the intense rays of the July sun when he developed sunburn blisters on his dorsal fin. The flotilla stopped in Deep Bay, near Denman Island, one of the Northern Gulf Islands, British Columbia (Namu still had 250 miles to travel before reaching his destination). Hewlett was dispatched to find an antidote in the form of zinc oxide lotion. When they were told why the ointment was needed, the pharmacists could hardly believe what they were hearing. As the salve was only packaged in two-ounce tubes, Hewlett had to purchase every tube he could lay his hands on. After mixing the zinc oxide with mineral oil, Goldsberry applied the ointment to Namu's blistered dorsal fin using a brush attached to the end of a bamboo pole.

Once U.S. Customs and Immigration had been cleared in Friday Harbor, San Juan Island, (which, considering the unusual nature of the import, was not without its challenges—was Namu livestock or perhaps whale meat?) and Namu was safely in U.S. waters, inquisitive pleasure boaters joined the bizarre flotilla as it made its way south. So many boats in the same vicinity creating high levels of motor noise caused a problem for researchers from Boeing Company's acoustic division, who were recording Namu's vocalizations for possible use in anti-submarine warfare.

Even before Namu arrived in Seattle, money started changing hands. While the convoy waited in Deep Bay, a couple of enterprising young boys spotted a moneymaking opportunity and offered to take people out in their boat to view the "attraction." Namu was already a headline act as journalists, including Emmett Watson of the *Seattle Post-Intelligencer*, impatiently waited their turn to use the only phone booth available for transmitting the eagerly sought news about Namu.

As the flotilla neared Deception Pass, the seething mass of water separating Fidalgo Island from Whidbey Island, on July 25, it slowed down to wait for a tidal change. Lining the bridge and banks of Whidbey and Fidalgo Islands, some seven thousand sightseers, many of whom had

Crowds watch for Namu on Deception Pass Bridge. *Wallie V. Funk Photographs, Center for Pacific Northwest Studies, Western Libraries Heritage Resources, Western Washington University–Bellingham.*

been waiting for three hours or more, jostled and hustled to find a spot from which to see the whale. Cars and motorbikes backed up for miles on either side of the bridge spanning the treacherous currents and swirling whirlpools below.

Among those jockeying for position on the bridge was a young college student, Ralph Munro, who was studying for a bachelor of arts degree in education and political science at Western Washington University. Along with a bunch of friends, he had driven down to watch the unusual procession. Although he could not reach the crowded rail for a better view, Ralph caught a glimpse of Namu and his entourage approaching the bridge 160 feet below. In years to come, this casual observer would play a much bigger role in the drama that would eventually bring an end to the capturing of whales in Washington State.

At 8:33 p.m. on a glorious Sunday evening, with the golden orb of the setting sun dipping behind the haze of the San Juan Islands, the flotilla passed under the bridge. As Namu rolled twice and smacked his powerful flukes, an uproarious cheer rose from the assembled crowd followed by a ceremonial blow from the foghorns of the accompanying vessels, the *Iver Foss* and the *Robert E. Lee.*

To the accompaniment of a brass band and a troupe of go-go dancers, water-skiers, planes and boats, Namu arrived at his new home at the Seattle Marine Aquarium three days later. The four-hundred-mile journey starting in his home waters of British Columbia had taken eighteen days.

Not everyone celebrated the arrival of Namu. Once again, demonstrators representing the "Free the Whale" movement shouted their objections and antagonized waterfront shop owners, who threatened to douse the troublesome activists with hoses.

Namu made front-page headlines around the world. Listeners to Bob Hardwick's radio station heard Namu's "voice" between breaks. Pilots of passenger jet planes arriving at Seattle Airport gave updates on his health. A dance called the "Namu" was launched, which included such innovative moves as the dorsal, the spray and the dive. Sweatshirts bearing Namu's image were sold in the shops alongside children's coloring books. Prestigious Lloyds of London was appointed the underwriters for Namu's insurers, providing a high-risk policy to cover loss by vandalism or natural death—but not escape.

In his first month at the Seattle Marine Aquarium, Namu gave his captor some anxious moments.[7] The latest attraction refused to eat the tempting morsels offered, his dorsal fin flopped to one side and takings at the box office fell. Fortunately for Griffin, these were temporary problems. Soon Namu's appetite returned, and his dorsal fin became more erect again as he spent less time on the surface of the water (one of the commonest causes of flopped dorsal fins in captive killer whales).

Box office receipts increased with more than five thousand people visiting the aquarium to view Griffin's exotic new prodigy, who starred in up to five shows a day. The crowds' favorite trick was when Namu leapt high in the air to take a salmon, which Griffin held out over the water from a tower. Admission prices were raised from $1.00 to $1.50 for adults, $0.50 to $0.75 for children. The newly formed company Namu Inc. sold trademarked items such as toys and sweatshirts. By the end of the summer, Griffin had cleared not only the $8,000 he paid for Namu but also the estimated $40,000 cost of transportation to Seattle.[8] A year later, the press reported that he had lost money on Namu and owed $50,000 plus.[9]

But this was just the start of the exploitation of Namu. A month after his arrival in Elliott Bay, Seattle, film producer Ivan Tors visited Pier 56 and made a deal for the production of a feature motion picture starring Namu. The main condition for the film's financial backing was that Griffin swam with the whale. The little boy who aspired to ride on the back of a dolphin was about to have his dream come true.

As they say, be careful what you wish for. When faced with the reality of joining Namu in the water, Griffin admitted in his book, *Namu: Quest for the Killer Whale*, that his confidence sagged. The business side of promoting the wonders of the whale along with his recent rise to fame and notoriety, which included being presented with the key to the city of Seattle, kept Griffin away from the waterside and time with Namu.

With his brother's encouragement, Griffin quickly overcame his fears. Before long, he was grasping Namu's shining dorsal fin while being towed through the water. The film producer was delighted—he had his coveted first-time footage of the feared killer whale and a human in the water together.

With the biggest hurdle overcome, the film company wanted to start filming in as natural a location as possible. Rich Cove, an area of clear, quiet water near Bremerton, was chosen. A couple of months after his arrival in Seattle, Namu once again entered the traveling pen and crossed Puget Sound, but this time without any of the "pomp and circumstance" that accompanied his journey from Namu. A twenty-four-hour security guard was set up to watch over the famous star, and a net to keep out unwelcome visitors was fitted across the entrance to the cove.

Griffin soon developed a rapport with Namu. Although he did most of the water work with the whale, the late Robert Lansing, the actor starring as the biologist who tries to convince people living in a hostile coastal fishing community that killer whales are not the deadly predators they fear, undertook some of his own stunt work.

Almost as though the film was playing out in reality and the public saw for themselves the whale's cooperative, playful behavior, a gradual change in attitude toward the long-feared creatures of the deep began. With *National Geographic* running a story on Namu in March 1966, killer whales were no longer seen as ruthless, bloodthirsty predators that would kill a man on sight.

Once filming had ended, it was time for Namu to leave the tranquility of Rich Cove. Soon he was back at the Seattle Marine Aquarium performing in the pen netted off from the polluted waters of Elliott Bay. But not for long.

Although he had been eating up to four hundred pounds of salmon a day, Namu's health deteriorated. He began showing little interest in food, abrasions appeared on his skin and his reactions became slower and slower. In response to an urgent call, Griffin left his home on Bainbridge Island, arriving at the aquarium to find Namu circling listlessly, his breathing erratic and shallow. Open cuts covered his body; the once tall proud dorsal fin flopped on one side yet again.

Worse was still to come. Griffin watched helplessly as Namu, deranged with pain, crashed against the side of the float before circling, increasing speed and breaching, only to smash into the float again. The impact of the whale's speed and weight damaged the steel cables underneath the float. Wires trapped the sick and injured animal. Unable to escape from the confining cables or the pain, Namu drowned on July 9, 1966, a year after arriving in Seattle.

Despite Goldsberry's assertion that there was no pollution problem at Namu's waterfront pen, an autopsy revealed that a type of bacteria known as *Clostridium perfringens*, which lives in the gut of both animals and humans, had been aggravated by the severe water pollution and sickened the whale, causing colic and delirium. Like so many other whales later captured for marine parks, a bullet was found lodged in Namu's blubber.

Growth rings in one of his teeth revealed that Namu was around seventeen years of age. He was a member of C1 pod (official designation C11) of the Northern Resident community, which inhabit the coast of British Columbia. His mother, Kwattna (C5), died in 1995 at the age of seventy-one. She was most likely the female seen following Namu when he was taken from his family and home waters. Koeye (C10), believed to be his sister born in 1971, was still alive as of February 2010.

The Associated Press reported that Namu's carcass would aid scientific study at Virginia Mason Research Center in Seattle. His skull was saved for collections at the Burke Museum of Natural History and Culture, University of Washington. By an ironic twist of timing, the film *Namu, the Killer Whale* (re-issued as *Namu, My Best Friend*) previewed at the Orpheum Theater in Seattle the same month that Namu died.

CHAPTER 4

THE ORIGIN OF SHAMU

SHAMU, SHAMU, SHAMU!" The steady hypnotic chant increases in volume, blasting through the 5,500-seater Shamu Stadium packed tight with excited, expectant humanity. Slick trainers sporting designer wetsuits wave their arms high above their heads in a concerted effort to pump up the adrenalin-fueled crowd. The loud staccato music and screaming voices rise in pitch and intensity as the charged audience, intoxicated by the heady prospect of proximity to a killer whale, awaits the grand entrance of Shamu. He (or she) will perform amazing acrobatic twists and turns along with dazzlingly choreographed aerial displays for the delight of the thrill-seeking public, avid for entertainment and value for money. Those seated close to the Plexiglass-walled tank laugh and giggle, some a little hysterically, in anticipation of the splash from a wave of chemically treated water soon to be set in motion by the impact of the powerful flukes of a trained killer whale.

There have been many "Shamus" over the years at SeaWorld locations in San Diego, Orlando, San Antonio and formerly Aurora, Ohio. But where did the trademarked name given to the Shamu shows at SeaWorld, the multimillion-dollar marine and theme park enterprise, originate?

The name Shamu is a mixture of "She" and "Namu" (meaning "friend of Namu"). Although Namu died alone, he did not spend all his time in captivity without company of his own kind. Three months after acquiring him, Griffin set off in search of a companion for the lone whale.[1] A considerable motivator was the sum of $20,000, the amount agreed on by the producers of *Namu, the Killer Whale* when cinematographer Ivan Tors expressed his wish to film a live whale capture.

Griffin and Goldsberry's experience with Namu showed that killer whales rarely attempt to break through or jump over nets. Goldsberry had already found that whales could be contained in a seine net, providing they had enough room to move.

After gathering their resources in October 1965, Griffin and Goldsberry were successful in finding and trapping fifteen killer whales in Carr Inlet, Puget Sound. The two men had pursued a pod of whales for several days by air and sea. Adam Ross, captain of the *Chinook*, a sixty-five-foot purse-seiner, joined the search. Ross was one of the men responsible for calling the two Canadian fishermen who captured Namu to inform them that Ted Griffin might be interested in the whale.

Although cinematographer Lamar Boren did not care whether a male or female was captured, Griffin and Goldsberry were keen to find a mature bull. With a tall prominent dorsal fin cutting through the water, that should have been easy. But the fleeing whales, which are capable of exercising clever diversionary tactics in the face of potential threats, had split up and were harder to see. Although their usual swimming speed is six to eight miles per hour, they can swim up to thirty miles per hour and cover seventy-five to one hundred miles a day. When Goldsberry called Griffin, intent on the pursuit of a single female, and told him that the pod was miles away near Point Defiance, Tacoma, Griffin realized he had been decoyed.

After Griffin rejoined Goldsberry, the pair tried herding the pod of whales into Quartermaster Harbor, on Puget Sound's Vashon Island, using firecrackers, also known as seal bombs (loud explosive devices to frighten seals away from fishing areas, now illegal in the United States) to scare and disorient the whales. The attempt was unsuccessful.

Faced with the threat of failure, the team returned to Gig Harbor to lick their wounds while the whales enjoyed a respite from the exhausting hunt. But the break was all too brief. Ross relayed a fresh report of whales under Fox Island Bridge, near Tacoma Narrows. Once again, Griffin set off by helicopter to find them. On this occasion he was successful—but not quite successful enough. Spooked by the whirring of the helicopter blades, the whales separated in different directions. Noting a large bull among the pod, Griffin kept the animal in his sights. But when the whales split yet again, the bull disappeared.

With no further sign of the bull, Griffin's attention turned to the smaller curved dorsal fin of a large female cutting rhythmically through the water.

When she surfaced below the helicopter, with the calculating, single-minded concentration of the hunter intent on his prey, Griffin aimed the harpoon rifle and fired. The barbed steel tip struck, entering the whale's abdomen.

With an orange marker buoy attached to the harpoon, the injured female struggled toward Carr Inlet. Accompanying her were two other members of the pod and the purse-seiner *Chinook*. Ahead, the film crew positioned its boat, ready to block the whales' exit. With the *Chinook* closing in behind, there was no escape.

Near shore, more whales had surfaced. Swiftly dispatching the net, the *Chinook* maneuvered into position, trapping those whales along with the harpooned female.

But again Griffin was outwitted. Something had gone amiss with the net. The orange marker buoy towed by the wounded whale suddenly disappeared. With the rest of the whales surfacing outside the net, the harpooned female fought to free herself from the agony of the shaft of cold steel embedded in her gut. After twisting and turning, she succeeded, and, with a final desperate surge of strength, pulled free of the harpoon line.

Griffin had lost another battle. With daylight fading and distressed whales scattering in all directions, he stood little chance of success before nightfall. But as he watched two whales surface, including a large female, he knew he had to make one final attempt. Instructing the pilot to take the helicopter down, Griffin aimed the harpoon rifle and fired. He hit the target. With darkness falling, the harpooned cow, dragging a line of orange marker buoys in her wake, was left to her own devices for the night.

Next morning, the *Chinook* and a second seining vessel were back, following the orange marker float. As the *Chinook* advanced and began to release its net, the whales panicked, making a final bid for freedom, but were cut off by a number of small boats speeding ahead of them. With the seining vessels working in tandem and the only other escape route blocked, the net closed around its victims, a cow and calf. Tors had his sought-after film of the capture of a live killer whale.

The following day, the travel pen that had transported Namu on his long journey south was back in service. The ever-diligent Boren, keen to film the transfer of the two whales to Rich Cove, waited with his camera. By now, her lung pierced by the harpoon, the wounded female's breathing became more spasmodic and labored as she struggled to dive and surface within the confines of the pen. Finally, after a long shuddering convulsion, she abandoned her desperate attempt to cling on to life, drowning as she sank slowly below the surface. Griffin admits in his book *Namu, Quest for the*

Killer Whale that he and Goldsberry made the decision to "conceal the loss." Using chain and anchor to weight her down, the female's carcass was sunk without ceremony. Griffin came clean about the attempt at secrecy after a reporter spotted him taking a whale to a Seattle rendering plant—but a different whale. Another had died during the hunt after being overdosed with tranquilizers.[2]

The orphaned calf continued alone to join Namu. Although initially she frolicked and played with her mate, before long she tried to ram the older male, both when he was alone and with Griffin on his back. His confidence shaken by the calf's aggression, Griffin found himself wondering what to do with his latest rather dangerous acquisition.

Fortunately for him, in 1964, SeaWorld opened a new facility in San Diego built on twenty-two acres in Mission Bay Park (by 1969, this had expanded to fifty-five acres) and was interested in obtaining a killer whale. After seeing film of the orphaned calf, SeaWorld agreed to lease, rather than buy, the little whale in case she did not survive. She was eventually purchased, according to the Associated Press, for the reported sum of $75,000.[3]

On December 20, 1965, cradled in a canvas sling with padded holes for her pectoral fins, the young female was flown by a Flying Tiger Line cargo aircraft 1,066 miles from Seattle to San Diego. She was accompanied in the cargo hold by veterinarians Dr. Pete Schroeder and the late Dr. David Kenney, SeaWorld's first veterinarian. SeaWorld wanted to call the little whale "Namu" and have the rights to the name, but Griffin refused. Instead the name "Shamu" was adopted and became the trademark name for the show.

To avoid the risk of dehydration, the two veterinarians sprayed water on Shamu to keep her skin wet during the flight. After landing at San Diego Airport, she was transported by truck to SeaWorld, arriving late that night.

Such a journey, following a traumatic capture, cannot have been anything other than stressful for an intelligent, cognizant marine mammal whose natural life is meant to be spent in the cool temperate waters of the Pacific Ocean. Up until the mid-1970s, orcas were secured in slings on long haul flights—with some losses. In one instance, Tula, who was captured off Malcolm Island, British Columbia, in July 1968 and transported to the Harderwijk Dolphinarium, Holland, endured a journey of sixty-eight hours. Although Tula survived the marathon journey, he died three months later of a fungal infection.

Abrasions sustained during transport, where the whales' pectoral fins and tail base were exposed to the pressure of their own weight in the stretcher, were a common problem on long haul flights. Once airlines started to charge by weight, rather than volume, whales were transported in specially constructed steel boxes filled with water. Some of the stress of the journey was eased by the animal's weight being supported by water and crushed ice to help prevent overheating. More recently, when transporting whales by air, marine parks have had to comply with the guidelines set by the International Air Transport Association (IATA).

To help Shamu adapt to her new environment, a dolphin named George joined her in the pool.[4] Soon Shamu was learning to earn her keep, cavorting and leaping for a reward of dead fish. Rocketing to fame, she became the star of *Shamu Goes Hollywood* as she streaked through the water, a trainer astride her back, to the theme tune of that notable television series *The Lone Ranger.*[5]

Shamu made history. Not only was she the first intentional live capture, but she was also the first whale to be flown in an aircraft and the first killer whale to perform at SeaWorld. In its first year of operation, more than 400,000 people visited the San Diego facility. From this adventurous and successful beginning, a whole new world of theme parks and entertainment burgeoned and a dynamic new industry was born.

The original Shamu performing at SeaWorld San Diego in 1967. *Photo Pat Hathaway.*

Today Shamu is marketed exorbitantly. Every opportunity is taken to capitalize on the legacy of the harpooned mother and orphaned calf. Shows such as *Dine with Shamu* and *Shamu Rocks*, which is advertised as having "more flash—and certainly more splash—than a rock concert" are designed to attract an unsuspecting public, unaware of the tragedy behind the name. While Shamu is performing the same routine up to five times a day, children clutching male and female SeaWorld Trainer Dolls and "Shamu Plush" soft, cuddly toys make their way toward the Shamu Express in Shamu's Happy Harbor.

Until recently, Shamu had a Webcam from which she (or he) could be viewed swimming around the barren, featureless tank. There are no kelp beds in which to forage or play, no subterranean, rocky channels to explore, no need for the sophisticated and highly evolved sense of echolocation to hunt for food.

In May 1970, SeaWorld expanded, opening another fifty-acre park in Aurora, Ohio (later sold to Six Flags in 2001, which in turn sold it to Cedar Fair—the park was largely demolished and closed down permanently in 2007 except for the "Wildwater Kingdom" water park). Unlike SeaWorld San Diego, with its warmer temperatures, the harsh winter climate prohibited year-round use of the Ohio park, which operated seasonally from May to September. Every summer, the "traveling circus" came to town. Shamu, SeaWorld's biggest attraction, was flown with other animals, dolphins and aquatic mammals the two thousand miles from San Diego to perform for the public, only to endure the stress and trauma of the long return journey by plane, crate and truck at the end of the short season. In May 1971, the press reported that during one such transfer, "Shamu was saved from possible death Sunday when a canvas sling tore as it carried the animal 30 feet above an asphalt pavement."[6]

Shamu also hit the headlines for different reasons in 1971. On April 19, Annette (Anne) Eckis, who worked as secretary to Kent Burgess, the director of SeaWorld's animal training department, rode Shamu for a publicity stunt.[7] Unlike the trainers, who wore wetsuits, Anne wore a bikini. A strong swimmer with some scuba diving experience, Anne practiced for the publicity stunt on Kilroy, a smaller, more docile whale. She wore a wet suit for her first practice ride on Shamu and fell off but swam to the edge of the tank without incident. She was unaware that training records showed that Shamu had been behaving erratically for over a month. Nor did she know that Shamu had reacted to two previous riders not wearing wet suits, one a Catalina swimsuit model and one a

SeaWorld trainer. She was even less likely to know about Ted Griffin's experiences with Shamu in Seattle.

On the second of three rides, a trainer noticed Shamu's tail fluttering, a sign of irritation. Anne slipped off Shamu's back during the third ride when Shamu failed to obey a signal. The whale turned and grabbed Anne's leg, pulling her around the tiny tank. One of the trainers jumped into the churning water and tried to rescue her, but Shamu continued to push Anne round as the girl struggled desperately for air. She managed to grab a pole from one of the trainers at the side of the pool but was forced to let it go as Shamu continued to thrash around with Anne's leg between her jaws. Within a few seconds, Anne managed to grab another pole while the trainers tried to pull her out. Eventually, Shamu's jaws were pried apart with the end of a pole, and Anne was released from the vice-like grip. She collapsed and was carried away on a stretcher, needing one hundred to two hundred stitches for the lacerations and puncture wounds she sustained.

In August 1971, four months after the potentially lethal attack on Anne Eckis, Shamu died of pyometra ("pyo" meaning pus, "metra" meaning uterus) and septicemia (infection of the blood),[8] a malady that affects unspayed cats and dogs. After having been traumatically orphaned as a calf, she had survived six years in captivity and earned SeaWorld millions of dollars in ticket sales and merchandize.

But the legacy of Shamu, the second Southern Resident to be captured, lives on. Just like any other replaceable commodity, when one Shamu dies, another awaits its cue from the smiling trainer standing in the wings of SeaWorld's wet, glitzy stage.

CHAPTER 5

THE BEGINNING OF AN INDUSTRY

Although Griffin and Goldsberry had little in common, they were both focused on one thing: catching killer whales. Each complemented the other with their skills. Goldsberry was a hardheaded commercial fisherman competent in handling boats and setting nets. Griffin had a talent for finding and catching orcas. Using boats, seaplanes, helicopters and any other means at his disposal, Griffin herded the whales toward where Goldsberry waited. Once entrapped by the nets, which could stretch up to three-quarters of a mile long, few whales attempted to escape.

A place that was to feature largely in Griffin and Goldsberry's quest for whales was Whidbey Island. One whale, at least, had a lucky escape in January 1966:[1] "Seattle (AP): A female killer whale…regained her freedom Sunday. Ted Griffin…said the nameless cow escaped when the purse-seine in which she was caught collapsed in a strong tide. The incoming tide swept the net to the head of the bay on the east shore of Whidbey Island."

Having gradually refined their hunting technique, and with lucrative orders for killer whales arriving from marine parks across the world, Griffin and Goldsberry set out to supply customer demand. There were no laws or regulations in effect with regard to the capturing of killer whales—it was free pickings for anyone who had the resources. Even so, sound knowledge of the sea, tides and currents was essential, as well as the ability and expertise to use a seine net. Finding whales, whether by sea or air, was not easy in such a large body of water as Puget Sound. To help them in their search, Griffin and Goldsberry had a network of watchers, including fishermen, scattered at different locations along the coast.

In February 1967, after being notified by the Coast Guard that killer whales had been spotted at Port Angeles, the first major capture of the Southern Residents took place.[2] With the assistance of a seaplane, a helicopter and the purse-seiner *Chinook*, Griffin and Goldsberry pursued and trapped fifteen whales in Yukon Harbor, near Seattle, early one evening. Because calves and juveniles were easier to handle, train and transport, the two men concentrated their efforts on capturing those. Maneuvering them onto canvas stretchers and flatbed trucks was less of a challenge. Lighter weight meant cheaper to ship.

As the capture team moved relentlessly toward their quarry, panic-stricken mothers fought frantically to save their calves while calves fought equally hard to stay with their mothers. During the violent process of trapping the whales in the nets and tearing the families apart, three whales died.[3] More fatalities would follow in the years to come.

After Griffin and Goldsberry had taken stock of their catch and selected three females and two males (believed to be members of K pod, the smallest of the Southern Resident population), the remaining seven whales were released back to the wild. Just how long it would be before they were hunted down again was anyone's guess.

Following capture, the whales were taken to the Seattle Marine Aquarium. George W. Klontz details the treatment of those animals captured in Puget Sound during 1967–68.[4] Before being lifted from the water to the boat deck, the killer whales were injected with dexamethazone, the dosage calculated according to body weight. An injection of pentylenetetrazol (metrazole) was also administered to offset the effects of physiological shock.

To avoid dehydration, water was sprayed constantly over the newly captured whales on their journey to the Seattle Marine Aquarium. Blood samples were taken from the ventral fluke vein, and a seven-day course of antibiotics was administered to each individual to offset the risk of infection from "the myriad of scrapes and cuts received before and during capture." A four-and-a-half-inch hypodermic needle was used to inject the whales in front of and to the side of the dorsal fin.

Captive whales were hoisted from the water by canvas slings and suspended in the air for five to ten minutes. The report states, "The effect of gravity was probably the biggest stress factor the animals had ever experienced." Whales that resisted and struggled during the transfer process were lowered back into the water for a few minutes before another attempt was made to raise them with as little jerking as possible. Finally, they were lowered onto inflated inner tubes with only a portion of their body weight supported by the boom.

On arrival at the aquarium, the whales were transferred to a tank waist-high in water. After the canvas sling was removed, two to four people standing in the water held twisted bedsheets underneath each animal to help support them for fifteen to thirty minutes. They all showed signs of disorientation, and great care was needed to stop them from rolling over and drowning. When a whale started to move, the trainers retreated to the side of the pool, and the water depth was increased to four feet. It was quite usual for whales and other marine mammals taken into captivity to circle their tanks emitting distress calls for the first couple of days.

On the second day, the whales were force-fed a mixture of homogenized herring, food supplements and vitamins through a rubber hose inserted in the throat. They were also offered dead herring by hand. Once acclimated and voluntarily feeding, they were given some basic training before being sold to various marine parks.

The five young orcas captured on this occasion—Walter, Ramu, Kilroy, Katy and Kandu—were soon traveling the seven miles to the Seattle Marine Aquarium. Katy, the smallest, was still a nursing calf. Along with a fourteen-foot juvenile male (Walter or Ramu), she was hoisted by crane onto the deck of a fishing boat and eventually deposited in the aquarium's shallow seal pool before being covered in wet sheets. To substitute for the loss of her mother's rich milk, she was tube-fed a special diet of homogenized whipping cream, Sustagen, ground herring and water three times a day. By adapting her diet on succeeding days, Katy was accepting whole small herring after ten days.

Following the first week of captivity, all the whales were blood tested and inoculated with 5cc erysipelas bacteria and 10cc *Clostridium perfringens*, Type D toxoid (Namu died as a result of *Clostridium perfringens* infection). Booster inoculations were given ten to twelve days later.

A month after the Yukon Harbor capture, the first of the whales left his home waters. Encased in the customary sling, Walter was transported by truck across the Canadian border on a four-hour journey to the city of Vancouver, British Columbia. Two attendants accompanied him, pouring buckets of water over his skin at regular intervals. Walter was on his way to the Vancouver Boat, Trailer and Sports Show,[5] where he was to spend ten days in a small display pool as one of the main attractions. On arrival, he was given more antibiotics and force-fed by pump. Walter was eating some live fish on his own, but as reported, "Walter's diet until

February 15 included seals, porpoise, large fish, and other whales, but now he settles for salmon, herring, and mackerel."[6] Such bold statements go to show how little was known about the different types of killer whales and their diets at that time.

During Walter's time at the boat show, attended by more than 100,000 people,[7] Ted Griffin set up an experiment to see if whales would communicate with one another by telephone.[8] The $150 call between the Vancouver Aquarium and the Seattle Marine Aquarium lasted an hour. Initially, the only response to Walter's squeaks came from two seals that barked in a nearby tank, but after about forty-five minutes, Walter's calls were picked up by two of the other whales still held at the Seattle Marine Aquarium. Knowing what is known now about the calls shared between members of the same pod, it is hardly surprising to learn that the whales "talked." Tape recordings of the "conversation" were sent to the Stanford Research Institute, California for further study.

When the exhibition ended, Walter was sold to the Vancouver Aquarium for an undisclosed sum. Accompanied by his captor, Griffin, Walter was trucked through the city of Vancouver before being hoisted once again by crane and lowered into his new home, the dolphin pool at Stanley Park, while the dolphins were re-housed indoors. A few days after his arrival, Walter was renamed "Skana" when aquarium officials realized that "he" was, in fact, a "she."

Soon after *her* arrival at the Vancouver Aquarium, a veterinary check was carried out on Skana to see if she was expecting a calf.[9] After draining the pool so that she was beached (a common husbandry technique used by marine parks and aquariums to administer injections and health checks), stethoscopes were run over Skana's chest, back and stomach to try to detect a heartbeat, or heartbeats. When nothing was heard, a second attempt to find signs of life was made by using an electrocardiograph machine. This test revealed as much as the first one—nothing.

While she was beached, Skana was vaccinated against entero-toxaemia and given a dose of equine roundworm medicine administered through a stomach pump. Blood samples were taken to compare her blood with that of human blood and that of Moby Doll. With the question still remaining as to whether she was pregnant, Skana was measured so that comparisons could be made a month later when she would endure the whole procedure once more.

If any captive whale can be considered a pioneering whale, that whale was Skana. In 1967, Paul Spong, a New Zealand psychologist, joined forces with researcher Don White to measure killer whales' visual acuity. After conducting hundreds of tests, from which Spong deduced that Skana's eyes were as sharp as any cat's, Skana suddenly started giving the wrong answers to Spong's questions and no longer cooperated.

Realizing that the lone whale, deprived of companionship and stimuli, needed more interaction, Spong changed his tactics.[10] Sitting beside her tank, he played his flute and rubbed her head and body with his hands and bare feet. Skana's reaction came as a surprise when she dragged her teeth across the tops and soles of Spong's dangling bare feet—the contact was a gentle enough hint to show that Skana could use her strength if she wished.

After recovering from the initial shock, Spong tentatively put his feet back in the water. Once again Skana approached open-mouthed, whereupon Spong automatically jerked his feet away. He repeated the same routine once more but this time held his nerve and curbed the urge to pull his feet out of the water when Skana approached. As soon as he stopped playing the game, Skana lost interest.

Spong worked with Skana for over a year and later wrote, "I concluded that *Orcinus orca* is an incredibly powerful and capable creature, exquisitely self-controlled and aware of the world around it, a being possessed of a zest for life and a healthy sense of humor and, moreover, a remarkable fondness for, and interest in, humans."

Along with his growing awareness of the intelligence and gentleness of the orca, Spong began to develop serious misgivings about keeping Skana in captivity. He shared these concerns with both the Vancouver Aquarium and the outside world and suggested a gradual release program to return Skana to the wild. Although his radical opinions raised the public's awareness and curiosity, the Vancouver Aquarium did not take so kindly to them. Orcas in aquariums and marine parks are big money-spinners and crowd-pleasers, funded by the public's never-ending lust for entertainment.

Sadly for Skana, Spong was denied further access to her and advised to check in to a psychiatric clinic. He chose instead to team up with Robert Hunter, one of the founders of Greenpeace. The renegade pair headed anti-whaling campaigns, which helped lead to the world moratorium on most whaling under the International Whaling Commission.

After moving to Hanson Island just off Vancouver Island in 1970 and setting up camp to study whales in the wild, Spong obtained a special land-use permit from the provincial lands office to establish a permanent residence as a research base. With a number of hydrophones situated in the area of the orcas' critical habitat, OrcaLab continues to collect acoustic data recording the whales' dialects to this day.

In 1968, Hyak II, a Northern Resident captured in April in Pender Harbor, British Columbia, joined Skana at the Vancouver Aquarium, although no offspring was produced from the union. In March 1969, the *Miami News*[11] carried a story about Skana, following the death of a dolphin named Splasher. Skana was thought to have killed the dolphin when teeth marks were found on the carcass. The claim was refuted by the Vancouver Aquarium, which stated that the dolphin had died from other causes and Skana had, in fact, tried to save the dolphin by supporting its weight at the pool's surface.

When Skana died in October 1980 after contracting a vaginal infection,[12] she had gained the dubious honor of being one of the longest living orcas in captivity—thirteen and a half years. At least she was spared the trauma of being transferred from one marine park to another, the fate of so many other captive orcas. Skana's name, which means "Killer Demon" in the Native American Haida language, was more recently carried by L79, a Southern Resident male born in 1989. Skana, along with his mother, Spirit (L22), and brother Solstice (L89) swam freely in the Salish Sea until listed as missing in the summer of 2013.

Like Skana, Ramu only spent a month at the Seattle Marine Aquarium before he was flown to Los Angeles Airport and transferred by truck to SeaWorld San Diego. Housed in the oldest of SeaWorld's killer whale facilities, a small kidney-shaped pool, Ramu took part in up to sixteen shows a day during the summertime. At the risk of being anthropomorphic (attributing human characteristics to animals), it is difficult to imagine the sheer monotony of performing the same routine time after time. But that was life for Ramu.

While Skana had exhibited her boredom with routine in a gentle way, simply refusing to cooperate, Ramu showed his boredom in a more threatening manner. The trainers refused to work with him because he grew so aggressive, and he was moved to a back pool until John Hall, a navy scientist who later became research director for SeaWorld, "rented" him for a year for a hearing study.[13] According to Hall, Ramu was a "fabulous whale." He was transferred to SeaWorld Orlando in 1975, where he remained for seven years until his death in January 1982. Fifteen years in captivity (one and a half years longer than Skana) afforded Ramu the questionable distinction of being the longest surviving orca in captivity at that time.

Kilroy (the whale Anne Eckis practiced on before her disastrous publicity stunt on Shamu) was also purchased by SeaWorld San Diego along with Ramu, for a reported price of $10,000 each.[14] When SeaWorld opened its park in Ohio in 1970, Kilroy was one of the orcas flown in to perform there during the summer months under the name of Shamu. A photograph in the *Lodi News Sentinel* shows an innocent chimp, Chester, with his head in Kilroy's mouth.[15] With his speed and agility, Kilroy earned himself the reputation as a top performer, excelling at the "wild ride."

Although marine parks claim that killer whales are rewarded with a treat of fish whether they perform or not, there is no such thing as a free lunch. The whales must earn their keep. After all, they are there to put on a show for the paying public.

The animals are taught a combination of different stunts. After being recalled to the trainer by a shrill whistle, a loop was placed in front of Kilroy. When he put his head through the noose, which fitted in front of his pectoral fins, he was rewarded with fish. Once the trainer was astride and holding onto the loop, Kilroy swam to the end of the pool and dived with the trainer on his back. When Kilroy reached the bottom of the pool, he heard another signal, "jump," and propelled himself upward with the trainer holding tightly to the loop. The exercise was repeated twice more. As soon as Kilroy went back to the shallower water, he was rewarded again with food. Kilroy, not much bigger than Katy when she was captured as a calf, spent eleven years performing at SeaWorld, dying in September 1978 of pneumonia, a common cause of death in captive orcas.

Little Katy, the smallest of the whales ripped from her mother while still a nursing calf, never left the Seattle Marine Aquarium. The infant choked on a stick three months after being captured, although according to a paragraph in Klontz's article,[16] this was not the actual cause of her death. Investigation with the use of a stomach tube failed to show that the stick was lodged in Katy's esophagus, and it was concluded that the barely weaned calf probably died of intentional drowning. Suicide in captive whales and dolphins is not unknown. Unlike humans, who breathe involuntarily, cetaceans are conscious breathers who must sleep with half their brain awake to avoid drowning.

Former trainer Ric O'Barry, now a dedicated animal rights' activist, (he drew attention to the barbaric Taiji dolphin drive with his Academy award–winning film *The Cove*) remains haunted by the memory of Flipper, the TV dolphin. O'Barry helped capture Kathy, one of the Flipper stars at the Miami Seaquarium, Florida, and has never forgotten how she gave up

Duwamish fireboat, South Lake Union Pier, Seattle. *Library of Congress.*

on life and died in his arms. O'Barry also witnessed suicidal dolphins while in Taiji when other pod members were being mercilessly slaughtered.

Two-and-a-half-year-old Kandu had the longest stay at the Seattle Marine Aquarium and almost never left it. The Seattle Fire Department was called early one morning when an aquarium employee arrived at work only to discover that a pump supplying water to the tank had stopped working during the night. The tank had drained, and Kandu was accidentally beached. With the aid of the fireboat *Duwamish*, berthed at a nearby pier, the tank was refilled and Kandu refloated.[17]

While waiting to be sold, Kandu underwent training with Geraldine (Jerry) Watmore, a former dolphin trainer from SeaWorld San Diego.[18] Initially, the trainer swam in the tank with Kandu, but as the whale grew bigger and began to push her around during her constant search for a reward (she ate sixty-five pounds of herring daily), it became too risky for Jerry to stay in the water with the whale. Kandu could have shown her strength in a much more drastic fashion but chose not to do so. This would not always be the case with killer whales in the years to come.

After almost three years, it was Kandu's turn to endure the trauma of transfer by crane, truck and airplane after being purchased by SeaWorld San Diego in December 1969.[19] She hardly had time to acclimate to the new environment housing other members of her pod—Shamu, Ramu and Kilroy—before she, along with the rest of the traveling circus, joined Kilroy at SeaWorld Ohio for the 1970 summer season.[20] It was the first, and last, season for Kandu—she died of pneumonia and liver necrosis in June 1971.

Griffin and Goldsberry continued to cast their nets far and wide—literally. A year after the Yukon Harbor capture, in February 1968, they captured twelve to fifteen whales in Vaughn Bay, near Tacoma, releasing ten to thirteen and keeping two, Lupa and Hugo.

After spending a couple months at the Seattle Marine Aquarium, Lupa, an adult female, was transferred to her new home at Coney Island's New York Aquarium, which opened in 1896. The New York Aquarium was the oldest continually operating aquarium in the world until October 2012, when Hurricane Sandy forced it to close for six months.

With a police escort for company, Lupa was accompanied along the Long Island Expressway before being lowered into the aquarium's "Polar Bay."[21] An article appeared in the *Milwaukee Journal*[22] describing how one of the keepers at the aquarium brushed Lupa's stained teeth, which, in the wild, would "routinely dismember a 100 lb. seal." Mention was also made of how gentle Lupa was for a creature with "such a fearsome reputation." She was popular with children, who in their innocence enjoyed her trick of squirting water at them. Trainers were less amused when she sent them scrambling for safety after snapping her jaws at them as they cleaned her tank.[23]

Life in Lupa's new concrete home was a short one—like others before her, she died six months later of pneumonia.[24]

Meanwhile, the young sprouter (the term used for an adolescent male whose dorsal fin is growing rapidly) Hugo spent a little longer in the Seattle holding pen before being transferred to the Miami Seaquarium in May 1968. Named after Hugo Vihlen, a Delta pilot from Homestead, Florida, they both had the number eighty-five in common.[25] Hugo Vihlen sailed the Atlantic alone in a six-foot sailboat in eighty-five days; for Hugo the whale, the number was less salubrious, representing the number of days from capture to arrival at the Miami Seaquarium.

For the first two years of his life there, the twenty-three-foot sub-adult was kept in two small pools known as the celebrity pool (now the manatee pool)[26] with a Pacific white-sided dolphin for company. Ric O'Barry, one of Hugo's trainers, turned his back on Hugo's tiny tank after making public his opinion that it was both bad and dangerous to keep whales in captivity.

Hugo was later moved to a newly built, larger pool to join Lolita, a young L pod female captured in the infamous 1970 Penn Cove capture. No one knew that they were both members of the Southern Resident community, and the two whales were initially kept separate, as there were fears that they would fight. After hearing them calling to each other constantly, the decision was made to move Hugo from the manatee pool to join Lolita in the Whale Bowl, where the pair performed their daily routines both together and apart.

After one of the trainers put his head a little too far into Hugo's mouth and ended up with ten stitches to his head and neck, Hugo was described by one newspaper as a whale that "would rather play than gobble sea lions and people."[27]

The only person Hugo had the opportunity to gobble was his trainer, who, dressed in a sea captain's outfit, rowed out to the middle of Hugo's pool with a dummy harpoon to imitate harpooning a whale, a sick trick if ever there was. Hugo was trained to capsize the boat and then "rescue" the floundering trainer by swimming underneath him. The trainer was then carried on Hugo's back to the side of the pool. Once the trainer was out of the water, Hugo collected the boat, oars, harpoon and trainer's cap and returned them to the

Lolita and Hugo at the Miami Seaquarium. *Photo courtesy Orca Network.*

Hugo and Lolita at the Miami Seaquarium. *Photo courtesy Orca Network.*

trainer, who then stepped onto Hugo's back to be carried around the pool. If the trainer fell off and tried to get out of the pool, Hugo pushed him away. The performance ended with another trainer creating a distraction by tempting Hugo toward another part of the pool with the offer of a reward.

Not long afterward, Hugo's performances were canceled after he clamped ahold of a trainer's raincoat.[28] Veterinarian Jesse White defended Hugo's behavior, saying that if the whale had wanted to bite the trainer, he could easily have done so. Someone who showed no fear of Hugo when she visited him in March 1973 was the popular Olympic Soviet gymnast Olga Korbut.[29]

In January 1980, Hugo began to exhibit signs of sluggishness.[30] Despite a diet reinforced with vitamin supplements and antibiotics, two months later, staff at the Seaquarium found him floating belly up in his tank. A necropsy revealed he had suffered a fatal brain aneurysm (massive hemorrhage). Before his death, he had rammed his head against the wall and viewing windows of the tank several times, on one occasion severing the tip of his rostrum. Jesse White sewed the severed rostrum back on, and Hugo carried on performing for the ever-waiting crowd.[31]

After his death, Hugo's carcass was hoisted from the pool and removed to an undisclosed location, believed to be the Dade County Landfill. Lolita was given no time to grieve for the loss of her companion. Like any top-billing star, she was performing the next day for her faithful public. No matter how great the tragedy, in true showbiz tradition, the show must go on…

For Griffin and Goldsberry, it was proving a bountiful year. In October 1968, they returned to Yukon Harbor, capturing twenty-five to thirty-three members of J and/or L pods.[32] Between twenty and twenty-eight escaped or were released, including one particular whale that in time would rise to iconic status. Later to be officially designated (J1), Ruffles was the first whale to be given an alphanumeric number and so named because of his huge, ruffled dorsal fin. On this occasion he was saved from captivity, as he was too big to transport. Ahab, Ishmael, Haida, Mamuk and Cuddles were not so lucky.

The Pentagon had been in contact with Griffin to discuss killer whales' suitability for use by the military. Dolphins were already in training for potential warfare operations. As the killer whale is the largest member of the dolphin family, it was thought likely that it, too, could be trained to recover dummy torpedoes from the firing range.

Ruffles (J1) in Admiralty Inlet, October 2010. *Author collection.*

Griffin was asked to supply two whales. On October 22, 1968, Ahab and Ishmael were on their way to the Naval Undersea Center, Point Mugu, California. Here they were housed in a circular concrete pool eight feet deep and fifty feet in diameter while waiting to undergo basic training.[33]

Ishmael, the smaller of the two at seventeen feet and 4,409 pounds, was moved to a forty- by sixty-foot floating pen in Mugu Lagoon in November 1968. After adapting to his new surroundings, Ishmael began his training. During the next few months, he learned to respond to a recall buzzer, retrieve an inflated ball and attached ring and allow human handling. He also learned to hold his breath and exhale when given an acoustic signal, follow a small outboard skiff and swim through a ten- by ten-foot gate. Ishmael's newly learned behaviors were put to the test in December 1969 when he was released into Mugu Lagoon. Having by now become semi-"institutionalized," his reaction to the open water was to retreat and return to the familiar territory of the floating pen.

By mid-January 1969, Ahab, the bigger of the two whales at nineteen feet and 5,500 pounds, had accepted handling and having his eyes covered. He learned to tow a swimmer, retrieve an inflated ring and respond to a recall buzzer. In October 1969, he was transferred to the Naval Undersea Center in Hawaii to take part in the Project Deep Ops program. After being flown by C-141 Starlifter aircraft, he was loaded by stretcher onto a flatbed truck and driven to Sag Harbor on the western end of Mokapu Peninsula, Hawaii, where the navy's complex of ocean pens open on to Kaneohe Bay and a channel to the sea. Ahab was then, in accordance with the usual procedure, hoisted by crane and lowered into the water.

In January 1970, Ishmael joined his pod mate Ahab in Hawaii.

After acclimating to the change of environment (between one and thirty days was allowed for this), Ishmael and Ahab began training. Just like Shamu's training for the "wild ride," the animals were taught to carry out a sequence of behaviors with food being the primary reinforcer. Conversely, food reduction was used as a motivator when an animal failed to cooperate. Ishmael showed a preference for mackerel, consuming 125 pounds a day. Ahab preferred bonito, eating 100 pounds a day.

Gate training can be a time-consuming process with cetaceans, and Ahab and Ishmael were no exception. Despite Ishmael having undergone gate training while in Mugu Lagoon, he had not retained what he learned. Efforts were made to crowd the whales through the gates using nets, but even if this method was successful on one day, it did not necessarily mean the whales would go through the gate on the next. Scraping their pectoral or dorsal fins on the gate parameters was an uncomfortable sensation they naturally preferred to avoid.

Once they had attained a satisfactory level of gate training, the two whales were trained to wear harness packs with tracking transmitters. With visual contact hard to maintain beyond two hundred yards from the training platform, the transmitters enabled trainers to stay close to their charges if control was lost during a work session. Ishmael and Ahab learned to swim into loops of rope later replaced with strapping material. As soon as this level of training was achieved, dorsal packs with bellybands were attached to the whales. The bands were tightened and secured using a cargo ratchet and locking mechanism. The actual harnessing of the whales was undertaken from rubber dinghies or training platforms.

The whales also had to be trained to take, and hold, a large yellow rubber mouthpiece. When Ishmael had undergone mouthpiece training, he had resisted by poking his tongue out. To prevent this undesirable behavior, he was rewarded for *not* moving his tongue.

When the whales had successfully achieved mouthpiece training, retractable practice grabbers were attached to the mouthpiece. Following a signal, they swam to the dummy torpedoes and clamped the torpedo in the grabber's arm. An inflated balloon then floated the torpedo to the surface. After swimming to the recovery boat, the animal received a reward.

When the time came for Ishmael and Ahab to undertake open water training, Ahab adapted more readily than Ishmael. It took another two months for Ishmael to adjust to working in the channel leading to the open sea.

Despite prevailing weather conditions in Hawaii necessitating cancellation of many open-water training sessions, by September 1970, Ahab and Ishmael had both attained open-ocean reliability status. They could swim in the open sea alongside a boat for a round-trip distance of ten to twelve nautical miles, about five times a week, at a speed of six to seven knots. However, the military believed they were too independent in spirit to be completely manageable.

This theory was tested, and proved, on February 19, 1971, when Ishmael did not respond to his underwater recall signal and swam away after an unsatisfactory training session. During the training session, he had exhibited frustration and annoyance by slapping his pectoral fins and flukes on the water after a dive of five hundred feet. It was not the first time he had shown this type of behavior when under pressure during training. After he swam away from the boat, the training session was discontinued. Although he responded initially to the recall signal and returned to the boat, he then turned and swam toward the open channel—and freedom. With the transmitter now signaling intermittently and only readable at close range, Ishmael took full advantage of the golden opportunity before him. Despite a concerted aerial and sea search over several days, the wayward whale was never seen again.

Having learned from their mistake, the navy fitted Ahab with a back-up transmitter on his pack. This enabled his captors to keep track of him when he went AWOL, setting off in a northwesterly direction along the Oahu coast for twenty-four hours and covering over fifty nautical miles. As a consequence of his unreliable behavior, Ahab was retired from sea trials in June 1971. He died three years later, a "sprouter" aged fifteen or sixteen, close to sexual maturity. The navy continued Project Deep Ops with Morgan, a pilot whale captured off the California coast at the same time as Ahab and Ishmael.

Back in Canada, the newly opened SeaLand of the Pacific in Oak Bay, just outside Victoria, British Columbia, had other plans for Haida. Nicknamed "Junior," the eighteen-month-old calf was first transported from the Seattle Marine Aquarium to Edmonton, Alberta, where he was put on display at the Edmonton Boat Show.[34] Once the boat show was over, "Junior" flew by Pacific Western Airlines from Edmonton to Patricia Bay Airport (now Victoria International Airport) before being transferred to the aquarium where he would be the star attraction. The aquarium planned to have a whale pool attached to a giant steel barge fitted with built-in tanks so that the public could view the exhibits from above and below the water. It also planned to start a breeding program.

Over a period of ten years, Haida had various female companions, the first being Nootka II, a member of K pod captured in Pedder Bay, near Victoria, British Columbia, in August 1973. Nootka II had previously been captured with the rest of K pod in February 1967 in Yukon Harbor. On that occasion, when three members of her family died, she was released, according to Canadian researcher Dr. Michael Bigg (Erich Hoyt refers to this in *Orca: The Whale Called Killer*). When she was unlucky enough to be caught a second time, her time in captivity was brief—she died nine months later of a ruptured aorta.

Haida's second companion was Chimo, an albino whale (a condition known as Chediak-Higashi syndrome) and a member of the Transient M pod captured in Pedder Bay, British Columbia, in 1970. Chimo died from her condition, or a complication arising from it, in November 1972. Haida grieved for the loss. He lay in the center of the pool, disinterested in offerings of food, for over a week. In an attempt to shake him from his lethargy, he was treated for a virus with a concoction made up of thirty-six bottles of ale, five-dozen eggs, ice cream and vitamins. To help raise his spirits, a flautist played music.[35]

Nootka III, a Transient orca from Q pod captured in Pedder Bay in 1975, was Haida's third mate. Like Nootka II, her time in captivity was short. She died of a perforated post-pyloric ulcer nine months later.

Haida's last companion was a bullet-ridden orphaned calf named Miracle, captured in 1977 in Menzies Bay, British Columbia. Although the two were kept in separate pens, Miracle and Haida communicated with each other until Miracle drowned in January 1982 after she became entangled between nets.[36]

SeaLand of the Pacific's plans to use Haida as a breeding male failed to come to fruition. His days ended when he died suddenly of a lung infection on October 3, 1982—three days before a federal permit came into effect to release him back into the wild in exchange for the capture of two other killer whales. Before the release, Haida was to have undergone a ninety-day training program that included learning how to catch live fish and an exercise program to build up his muscles and stamina.[37] His carcass was towed out to sea and sunk.[38]

The loss of Haida following Miracle's death earlier the same year and that of others before her provoked the environmental group Greenpeace to call for an independent inquiry. The group had already set up camp in the proposed capture area, Pedder Bay, and intended to disrupt the hunt. Due to the controversy and unwelcome publicity focusing the wrong sort of attention on the aquarium, SeaLand decided to abandon the imminent capture plan.

In his book, *Orca: The Whale Called Killer*, Erich Hoyt talks of his affection for Haida, whom he interacted with in a spontaneous game of "pass-the-seaweed-back-and-forth." This innocent exchange was a far cry from the trick he was expected to perform with a trainer pretending to pour gasoline into his mouth. His trained response to this ignominy was to copy the noise of an outboard motor while he swam around his enclosure.

Hoyt also talks of Canadian researcher Graeme Ellis's encounter with Haida in 1968, when the young male was "enthusiastic, the most responsive and eager orca of the captives I'd seen." After visiting Haida in 1975, Ellis said, "A captive whale has only one year, maybe two, before his mental health starts going downhill."

Mamuk, a juvenile male, survived until June 1974 after being taken to Sea-Arama Marineworld, Galveston, Texas, which opened in 1965. Competition from the more tourist-oriented SeaWorld Orlando contributed to its closing in 1990. Sea-Arama claimed that Mamuk was the only killer whale in captivity between the East and West Coasts. Here he performed in up to five shows a day, at one time suffering the indignity of a ridiculous pair of goggles perched on his rostrum.

Cuddles, the smallest of the captured whales, was destined to be the U.K.'s first captive orca and the first Southern Resident to make the long transatlantic crossing by air from Seattle to London. Accompanied by veterinary surgeon David Conrad Taylor and several attendants, Cuddles was transported in a large tank to London Airport in November. After being discharged from the cargo hold, he was driven another 250 miles by "pantechnicon," a type of furniture removal van, complete with the glory of a police escort, to Flamingo Park Zoo, Pickering, Yorkshire.[39] The zoo, founded by Pentland Hick in 1959, was later sold to Scotia Leisure Ltd., a company dealing mostly with package tours and bingo halls.

On arrival at Flamingo Park Zoo, Cuddles was lowered into a small pool with bottlenosed dolphins for company, a poor substitute for his close-knit

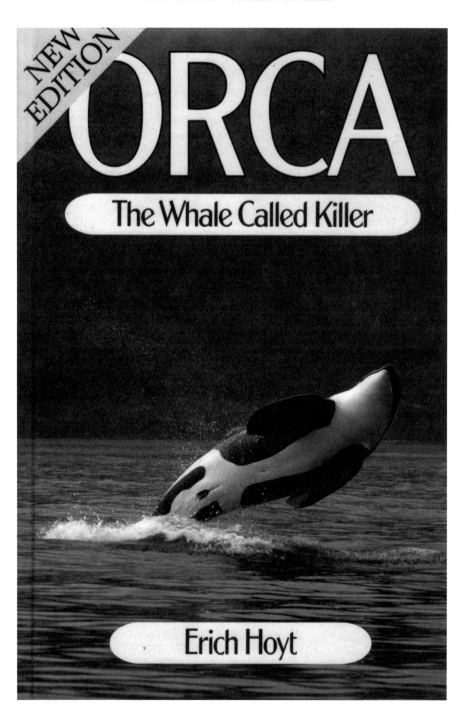

Courtesy of Erich Hoyt.

family unit. In an effort to alleviate his loneliness (which was displayed by the whistles Cuddles emitted at night), well-meaning zookeepers played a selection of pop music to him.[40]

The arrival of an orca on British soil was a huge attraction. Although orcas are found in all of the world's oceans, the daunting logistics of the Atlantic ocean and the Royal Fish Law of 1324 affording the Crown exclusive rights to all whales (classed as "fishes royal"), and the Whaling Industry Regulation Act of 1934 prohibiting the capture of any cetacean within two hundred nautical miles of the British coast, made obtaining such exotic creatures in home waters impossible.

An even greater novelty than Cuddles would be a baby whale. Using Cuddles as a donor, attempts were made to artificially inseminate Calypso, a member of the A5 Northern Resident pod captured in Pender Harbor, British Columbia, in December 1969. She was held temporarily at Cleethorpes Zoo and Marineland in Humberston, Yorkshire (also owned by Hick), while repairs were made to the pool she was to inhabit at Marineland in Antibes, France. The effort at artificial insemination was unsuccessful. Calypso died in December 1970 at Marineland, one year after her capture and thousands of miles away from home.

Meanwhile, Cuddles, who was suffering from intestinal ulcers and internal bleeding, had become increasingly aggressive. Doug Cartlidge, Cuddles's trainer, states:

> *The story of Cuddles is a sad one. No one really knew how to look after an orca, and they were treated just like dolphins. The aggression he showed was never really treated; staff just moved away from close contact and took greater care around him. I took over after a number of other trainers and worked with him for around a year before he was moved to Dudley* [Zoo]. *We simply put a net in the pool if we had to do any work in it. He had grabbed a few trainers but not caused serious injury, just held them for a while and took them to the bottom of the pool. I left after we had nursed him for weeks when he was passing blood daily, and the pool would be red with blood. The management said they had to move him to Dudley because all the media work had been done and the season was about to start…They moved him and I left for Windsor* [Safari Park]. *Unfortunately, the history of aggression from Cuddles was never passed on to other staff.*[41]

In May 1971, Cuddles was transferred to a small pear-shaped pool just over forty-nine feet long by nineteen feet wide by eleven feet deep at Dudley

Zoo in Worcester, an area known as the "Black Country" due to heavy industrialization during the Victorian era. In his novel *The Old Curiosity Shop*, Charles Dickens describes how factory chimneys "poured out their plague of smoke, obscured the light, and made foul the melancholy air." According to press reports, Don Robinson, the zoo's managing director, survived an attack by Cuddles when he was dragged into the pool, necessitating Robinson being rushed to Dudley Guest Hospital suffering from shock and injuries to his head and leg. Although Cartlidge believes this was a publicity stunt, it moved a member of Parliament in the House of Commons to call for the introduction of proper regulations to cover the feeding and custody of whales in captivity.

A British Pathé News clip shows footage of Cuddles, the killer whale, taken in 1969 at Flamingo Park Zoo.[42] The description reads, "We see various shots of Cuddles, the killer whale, in a pool. Her trainer, Geraldine Watmore, gets Cuddles to do several tricks, like pushing a ball through the water. Geraldine gives Cuddles a fish then brushes the whale's teeth with a large toothbrush. Geraldine throws a spanner into the water and Cuddles brings it back to her. More tricks, with the whale begging for fish…Geraldine is seen in the water with Cuddles—she gives Cuddles a kiss." Geraldine (Jerry) Watmore was the trainer who spent time with Kandu at the Seattle Marine Aquarium.

Such was life for Cuddles, not even afforded his correct gender, retrieving spanners and begging for food. In January 1973, he suffered abuse at the hands of mindless vandals who aimed a twelve-foot spear at their defenseless target before pelting him with a spate of rocks and bricks.[43]

Later that year, Cuddles was put up for sale at a price of $82,500[44] when the zoo ran into trouble for falling foul of building regulations. The whale and dolphin pools at Dudley Zoo had originally been designed as sea lion and seal pools. When the walls were built up to create more depth, they contravened the local planning laws. The zoo was ordered to return the pool to its original size but was not prepared to spend money to re-house Cuddles, who was under orders to be moved by April 1.

After breaking a rib and sustaining an infection from an abscess, Cuddles (scheduled for transfer to Nice, France) died in February 1974[45] in the shadow of the collieries and factory chimneys of the Black Country, six thousand miles away from the deep blue waters of the Pacific Ocean where he was born.

In some ways, 1969 brought a temporary reprieve for the Southern Resident community—but not for the Northern Residents in Canada, where more captures took place.

That is not to say that no whales were caught in Washington waters. Griffin and Goldsberry had customers from across the world willing to pay large sums for such a valuable asset. Continuing their never-ending search to satisfy waiting customers, in April 1969, they pursued and captured eleven more whales in Carr Inlet, Washington. Two were kept and the rest released.

Ramu II, a nineteen-foot male, was flown by Qantas 707 jet to San Francisco, followed by the long haul flight to Brisbane, Australia, for transfer to Marineland in Queensland.[46] He died just over a year later. The *Montreal Gazette* reported that Ramu, who had been purchased for $20,000 and was the largest killer whale in captivity, had developed a gastric ulcer.[47] His female companion (official designation SEQ-OO-C6901) died shortly after her capture.

In October 1969, Penn Cove on Whidbey Island became the focus of attention for Griffin and Goldsberry when seven to nine whales were captured. Six to eight either escaped or were released. One whale died—another casualty added to the mounting tally.

Little did anyone know that the brief foray into Penn Cove was to be the prelude to a much bigger controversial capture the following year, one that would have far wider reaching implications than anyone could have foreseen.

CHAPTER 6

THE GREAT WHALE HUNT

The year 1970 proved to be the peak capture, or "cropping," year for the Southern Residents. Although Canadian federal laws were passed in 1970 to prevent harassment, capture or killing of killer whales except for restricted permits to Canadian captors, no such protection existed in Washington State. Unlike their Canadian cousins, the Northern Residents, the Southern Residents remained vulnerable. A bill introduced at the last state legislative session to give greater protection to marine mammals had failed. One of those who opposed it was Ted Griffin.[1]

The closest the Southern Residents came to enjoying protection was when, following an extensive public hearing in June 1970, conservationists and commercial groups agreed that some type of marine mammal management was required. The Legislative Interim Committee on fish and game voted unanimously for the Department of Game to take on the responsibility for the management of marine mammals in Washington State. Although nobody at the time knew how many killer whales there were in the Puget Sound area, Goldsberry was quoted in an article titled "Notes on the Natural History of the Killer Whale *Orcinus orca* in Washington State" as estimating that the annual killer whale population in Puget Sound and surrounding waters was 250 to 300. In the same article, marine mammalogist Dale Rice stated, "The Puget Sound population of *Orcinus orca* is probably the densest in the world."[2]

January 1970 found Griffin and Goldsberry moored up in Hudson Harbor, Port Townsend, with a fleet of support vessels. The pair planned to spend six weeks in the area searching for killer whales. Griffin, his phone number chalked up on a board at the marina, put the word out for anyone who sighted whales to call him.[3]

He didn't have long to wait. The following month, he and Goldsberry captured six to fourteen whales in Carr Inlet.[4] They released all except one, which was kept at the Seattle Marine Aquarium.

Throughout the spring and summer, Griffin and Goldsberry continued their quest for whales. In late July, they struck it lucky when an estimated two hundred were spotted off Friday Harbor, San Juan Island.[5] During the summer months, the Southern Resident orcas spend much of their time foraging, playing and socializing around the San Juan Islands, a favored area for Chinook salmon.

Since the original sighting, the large pods of whales (also known as a superpod) had been moving south, with Griffin and Goldsberry in pursuit. Two weeks later, one of the blackest days ever to hit the Southern Resident population occurred when about one hundred whales, composing almost the entire clan (one whale was later captured off Bainbridge Island), were herded into Penn Cove on Whidbey Island. The *Seattle Times* reported that "workers from the Seattle Marine Aquarium tightened two nets around a group of up to several dozen killer whales captured in Penn Cove, Whidbey Island yesterday."[6]

Whidbey Island measures approximately forty-five miles long and twelve miles wide. It snuggles between the Olympic and Cascade Mountains and forms the northern boundary of Puget Sound. Access to the mainland is via Deception Pass Bridge at the island's north end and by Washington State Ferry service from Clinton to Mukilteo at the southern end. The pretty little community of Coupeville, one of Washington's oldest towns, was founded in 1853 by Captain Thomas Coupe after he claimed 320 acres on the south shore of Penn Cove in 1852. The redwood-constructed house that Captain Coupe built on Front Street in 1854 still stands, although it has been moved farther back because of erosion of the bluff on which it perched. The view across the calm waters of Penn Cove is breathtaking, especially on a clear day when the sun highlights the snowcapped magnificence of Mount Baker rising to more than ten thousand feet.

The surrounding landscape is gentle with mellow sandstone bluffs contrasted by red-barked madrona trees gracing the shoreline. The cove is named after a friend of Master Joseph Whidbey and Captain George Vancouver, who discovered Whidbey Island during their explorations of the Pacific Northwest in 1792. At one time, it was home to a number of Native

Mount Baker from Penn Cove, Coupeville, Whidbey Island. *Author collection.*

American temporary settlements and three permanent villages. In bygone days, shellfish provided an important contribution to the tribes' diets, and today Penn Cove mussels are world famous.

Looking at the peaceful waters and quiet town, now a popular tourist destination, it is difficult to imagine the horror of that summer day when the Southern Resident killer whales were driven into the cove. The event has been well documented over the years, and though the full details may have become a little clouded through the mists of time, the basic story remains the same.

All three Southern Resident killer whale pods—J, K and L—were in Admiralty Inlet on the west side of Whidbey Island heading north, probably on their way back to the San Juan Islands, when the pilot of a spotter plane saw rhythmically rising and diving dorsal fins below.[7] Gathering their formidable resources together, Griffin and Goldsberry were soon in full pursuit. Buzzing aircraft dive-bombed the fleeing whales while speeding boats drove them in the opposite direction toward the southern tip of Whidbey Island and Holmes Harbor. Once in the mouthpiece of the narrow, sheltered harbor, the whales would be trapped.

Because sound travels much faster underwater, the impact on marine mammals is intensified. Using acetylene torches, the ruthless hunters lit and tossed "seal bombs" into the water in rapid succession to frighten and disorient the beleaguered whales fighting to evade the noisy boats. For the whales, it was an all-too-familiar scene. By now, many had been captured before, some more than once.

With the imminent threat of the imprisoning nets closing in, the whales set up diversionary tactics by splitting into two groups, confusing the capture team and slowing them down. While some of the terrified whales turned east as decoys, many of the mothers and calves headed north toward Deception Pass and the open sea. But they were no match for the spotter plane's aerial advantage and the fast pursuit boats, which overtook the frantic mothers and calves on their flight to freedom. With their escape route through Deception Pass blocked, the whales were forced into the deepest part of Penn Cove, near the village of San de Fuca, from which there was no escape.

With the aid of the sixty-five-foot purse-seiner *La Touche* (since renamed *Commencement*) from Tacoma, owned by Matt Vodanovitch Jr., Griffin and Goldsberry's crew struck, encircling one group of whales with strong mesh nets. The second group was captured later that evening. Because of their lifelong family attachment, those whales that were still free followed their natural instincts and returned to join the rest of the pod. No great effort was needed by the orca cowboys to bring the remaining whales into the captors' waiting nets.

1970 Penn Cove capture site and former Standard Oil dock. *Author collection.*

Top: The historic Captain Whidbey Inn, Coupeville, built in 1907. *Author collection.*

Bottom: Lassoing whales, 1970 Penn Cove capture. *Wallie V. Funk Photographs, Center for Pacific Northwest Studies, Western Libraries Heritage Resources, Western Washington University–Bellingham.*

Next pages: Trapped whales, 1970 Penn Cove capture, Coupeville. *Wallie V. Funk Photographs, Center for Pacific Northwest Studies, Western Libraries Heritage Resources, Western Washington University–Bellingham.*

Photographs taken at the time of capture and examined years later by Canadian researcher Dr. Michael Bigg confirmed that all three pods, J, K and L, were present. At least twelve of the whales were between the ages of two and five years, just the right age and size for training and transportation to the eagerly awaiting marine parks.

The Captain Whidbey Inn, a romantic getaway on Whidbey Island with a history dating back to 1907 when Judge Still and his workers laid the first timber of the log inn, enjoys an unparalleled view across the tranquil waters of Penn Cove. But on that day, the waters churned and boiled white with agitated whales fighting to escape from the confining nets. Their desperation and terror was all too apparent as they spy-hopped repeatedly, raising their strikingly colored black-and-white heads from the water, coupled with high-pitched shrieks and cries echoing across the usually tranquil cove. A floating pen was set up to corral and separate the mothers and calves. Piercing, screaming vocalizations rent the air as the trapped whales thrashed and twisted in confusion, fear and panic. It was a sight and sound that would haunt the local residents forever.

Longtime resident Lyla Snover, who lives on the shoreline of Penn Cove, has never forgotten the incessant cries. She recalls clearly how her children asked, "Why are they crying? They're crying," as the whales' plaintive calls carried across the cove. "It was terrible, just terrible—like a prison camp, it was awful," Lyla said, "and I think everybody that remembers it will tell you that. It was just one of the most horrible things I've witnessed in my life."

John Colby Stone, whose parents ran the Captain Whidbey Inn, ferried Wallie Funk, editor and former co-owner of the *Anacortes American*, *Whidbey News-Times* and *South Whidbey Record*, out to the walkway raft in his eleven-foot aluminum boat, leaving him there to photograph the captured whales. No other member of the press was permitted to cover the story.

During the next six hours, Funk used up thirty rolls of film. Throughout the filming, he remained the professional photojournalist, and it was not until he had completed the assignment that he stepped back with a sense of outrage. Of all the historic events Funk has covered and the famous personalities he has been privileged to photograph during his colorful career, including five U.S. presidents, the Beatles and Mick Jagger of the Rolling Stones, the Penn Cove captures remain one of his most vivid memories. Stone, too, remembers the sadness of the event, hearing the cries of the whales and seeing their distress as their families were torn apart.[8]

One particular orca would stay in Stone's memory forever. Amid the chaotic mêlée of whales, a large male with a distinctive rippled dorsal fin headed toward his small boat, seemingly on a collision course. Stone changed course rapidly just as the tip of the huge dorsal fin submerged off the bow, reemerging once again off the stern. As Stone headed for the dock, Funk waved both arms and shouted, "Did you see that?"

Stone cried, "Yes, Mr. Funk, I saw it."

"Goddamn it," was the exasperated reply. "I'm out of film."

Some thirty years later, Stone encountered the same whale, Ruffles (J1), while boating in the San Juan Islands. Shutting down the engines, Stone watched Ruffles swim alongside his boat, the *Cutty Sark*. The big male rolled slowly over to one side, his knowing eye fixed on Stone. Did Ruffles remember him from those days in Penn Cove? Stone will always wonder.

Soon, about twenty-five whales were corralled in two net pens about one hundred yards long and fifty yards wide—fifteen in one pen, ten in the other. Those that remained free stayed outside the nets, about two hundred yards away, restlessly patrolling the outskirts of the pen. The capture team had already started pushing some of the large males away through devised breaks in the netting to reduce their selection to the smaller females and calves two to five years old, between eleven and fifteen feet long. Griffin had orders for half a dozen whales to fulfill; he did not want nursing whales or any less than ten feet long.

Captain John Colby Stone at the helm of the *Cutty Sark*. *Author collection.*

Dixie Lee Ray, governor of Washington from 1977 to 1981. *Photo courtesy Harold "Scotty" Sapiro, Washington State Archives.*

While Griffin's actions were creating mayhem for the whales in Penn Cove, he also drew criticism from an old adversary, Dr. Dixy Lee Ray (1914–1994), a marine biologist and director of the Pacific Seattle Aquarium from 1963 to 1972. Ray was later appointed the seventeenth, and first female, governor of Washington State from January 1977 to January 1981. She had challenged Griffin in January 1966 when he proposed a million-dollar aquarium for Seattle. Now she was launching a strong attack on him for taking whales for personal profit. She accused him of posting signs at marinas and offering rewards of $1,000 per whale that he, Griffin, then sold for $15,000 each.[9]

Ray advocated that the whales be protected by the State Game Department to bring a stop to the capture trade and exploitation for profit. She spoke of the death of Namu and others and the law against harassing animals, vowing to determine if it applied to whales. Griffin supported state laws to protect marine mammals, he said, as long as they allowed certain animals to be taken for public display or scientific research, without jeopardizing the resource.

Ray had a powerful ally in James Scripps, of the Scripps League newspaper chain. After flying over Penn Cove and seeing the plight of the whales, Scripps also criticized Griffin's methods and expressed interest in donating to a fund that would campaign for legislation to protect killer whales in the future.[10]

While the ongoing drama played out on the water with curious boaters and pleasure craft maneuvering nervously away from the nets as the whales smacked their flukes, breached and spy-hopped (described by the press as "one of their most interesting routines"), officials from the Department of Game whiled away the time in their boat, drinking beer.[11]

Whidbey News-Times reporter Mary Syreen and her husband took their fourteen-foot boat out to photograph the whales. But for Mary, as for so many people, her excitement was soon replaced by sadness as she watched the whales outside the nets keeping vigil and heard the plaintive crying of the calves calling for their mothers.

There was just as much interest in the whales on land as on the water, as more than one hundred cars lined the highway from San de Fuca to Kennedy's Lagoon. Motorists were undeterred by "No Parking Anywhere" signs and left their cars by the roadside while going in search of a better viewpoint to marvel at the unusual scene. Locals and tourists alike, some setting up chairs along the perimeter of the cove, peered through binoculars and clicked cameras at the biggest marine spectacle Whidbey Island had ever seen.

Opinions on the capture were divided. Some people were appalled. One woman remarked that she wished all the whales would get together and smash the nets and boats. Another said it was wrong to capture such beautiful creatures and force them to live in tanks, where many died early. Another spectator likened the scene to "shackling Sampson." Yet another said there should be a law against it, which there was not.[12] The only requirement to capture killer whales was a netting license from the Department of Fisheries. At the time, there were two separate departments in Washington State: the Department of Fisheries (food fish), under an appointed director, and the Department of Game (game fish), under a six-member commission.

But not everyone was opposed. Despite the objections of many, prejudice against wild killer whales still existed. After all, they were competitors for salmon. Two young teenagers said the whales should be sold, a local resident said he didn't care about them being captured so long as they weren't mistreated or killed and others said it was alright to capture whales providing such captures did not upset the ecology.

One group of concerned citizens sent a telegram to U.S. secretary of the interior Walter J. Hickel protesting the inhumane capture of killer whales for commercial purposes. The high mortality rate of captive whales was raised and a request made that the whales, as a vanishing species, should be protected along with other wildlife. The U.S. Department of the Interior's Fish and Wildlife Service replied that the federal government did not have jurisdiction over mammals in state waters. It was suggested that those who signed the petition should contact the Washington State Department of Game, which was seeking legislative steps to enable it to take charge of killer whale captures in the state.[13]

On Monday, August 10, Griffin made his first selection: a young, sixteen-foot female. After successfully lassoing the animal, the constricting rope was tightened around her body. Half a dozen men on the dock dragged and pulled the young female toward divers waiting to maneuver her on to a canvas sling. Overseen by a representative from the Department of Game, she was tied to a skiff and hauled to the old Standard Oil dock at San de Fuca to undergo the usual procedure. The sling was hooked on to a crane, hoisted from the water, suspended in the air and lowered onto a flatbed truck owned by M. Wieldraayer, a landscaper from Oak Harbor, ready for transit to the Seattle Marine Aquarium. Griffin accompanied the whale on the drive down through Whidbey Island for the ferry crossing from Clinton to Mukilteo, provoking considerable excitement and curiosity along the highway and among the ferry passengers. A whale on the ferry was hardly a day-to-day occurrence.[14]

A small flotilla, including a couple motor boats and two fishing boats (the sixty-foot purse-seiner *Pacific Maid* owned by Peter Babich, one of the two men who informed Griffin about Namu, had joined *La Touche*) congregated in Penn Cove to continue with the work of selecting more whales from the two dozen or so still waiting in the pens.

While the whales awaited their fates, a drama of a different kind erupted. During a frenzied attempt to reach the calf from which she had been forcefully separated, a twenty-foot female became entangled in the nets and drowned.[15] Such a noteworthy media event could only add to the rising tide of dissent, engendering the public's sympathy further and fueling the heightened anger and distaste for the capturing of killer whales. Although they might not yet realize it, the orca cowboys were now on borrowed time.

The last helpless victim to be taken away to a new life far removed from her family was Lolita (also known as Tokitae), the only surviving Southern Resident still alive in captivity. Pixie Maylor, a resident of Oak Harbor, recounted, "There was a bunch of us who went down every day, and it's the worst thing that I've ever seen in my life. It should never have happened. The whales cried. We watched them load them and saw them specifically load a small one in the back of a truck. I think it was probably Lolita and she cried and cried and cried the whole way. It's a sound you don't forget, you just don't. I'll never forget it."[16]

Someone else who will never forget either is diver John Crowe, then a young man of eighteen. It was his job to help get the little whale on the stretcher and flatbed truck. Crowe, who had already broken down but carried on working, will never forget hearing Lolita's heart-rending cries as she was torn from her family and home waters. Nor will he forget how

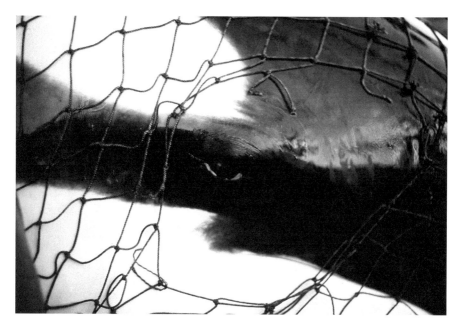

A bloodied helpless victim (possibly Lolita) of the 1970 Penn Cove capture. *Terrell C. Newby, PhD.*

the rest of the whales milled and circled restlessly fifty yards from shore, spy-hopping constantly in their desperate attempts to track the fate of their lost relative.

As the truck drove away and the little orca's cries faded in the distance, the remaining whales gave a collective sigh of despair as they turned from the shore and swam slowly away from the cove. Having had their tightly bonded families ripped apart, there was nothing left but to return to the open sea, grieving their irreparable losses.

With the last whale dispatched from Penn Cove and Griffin and Goldsberry's two-week sojourn at an end, the public's attention turned to Seattle. Eight whales, including the one captured off Bainbridge Island, were now held in two tanks at the Seattle Marine Aquarium awaiting shipment to marine parks around the world. Griffin and Goldsberry had orders from Texas, Japan, Australia and England at the reported price of $20,000 per whale. One female would stay at the Seattle facility for display, replacing Kandu I, captured in February 1967 and sold to SeaWorld San Diego in December 1969.[17]

The aquarium's valuable acquisitions were watched around the clock and each whale fed twenty-five to sixty-five pounds of herring daily.

They were all injected with antibiotics in preparation for their future lives in captivity.

While ticket sales at the aquarium swelled, sympathy for the whales grew. In addition to letters of complaint to local newspapers, a notice organized by Progressive Animal Welfare Society (PAWS), formed in 1967 to prevent cruelty to animals and promote legislation to protect them, was posted around town calling for a public protest against the inhumane treatment of whales at Pier 56 at noon on Saturday, August 22. About fifty people carrying signs such as "Killer Whales are not killers," "Why, why must they be caged?" and "Stop Exploiting our Whales" marched back and forth for an hour in front of Griffin's "Killer Whales & Seal Show" sign at Pier 56. The picketers gave full voice about the possible extinction of the whales coupled with condemnation of Griffin and Goldsberry for causing the death of the mother trying to reach her calf.[18]

The two men were not contrite. While agreeing that whale hunting should be controlled by legislation, they remained defiant, deriding any possible extinction of the species. They argued that representatives from the Department of Game had overseen the hunts and claimed that not only were the whales happy in captivity, but they also made a valuable contribution to entertainment and research.

The focus of attention did not stay on the Seattle Marine Aquarium for long. Although Griffin and Goldsberry had removed all their equipment from Penn Cove, they left a tragic legacy behind.

In early September, a dead calf washed up in front of the home of Ed Smith at Good Beach on Penn Cove.[19] The bold, beautiful white coloration was a sickly yellow; tallow flowed from a puncture wound in the calf's side.

In November, two more dead calves, measuring eight to ten feet, washed on shore at San de Fuca beach, near the capture site. Their bellies had been slit and weighted down with heavy rocks in a clumsy attempt to stop the carcasses from floating to the surface. Island County road crews removed the rotting carcasses to a burial pit near Oak Harbor following complaints by local residents.[20]

Ray, as a marine biologist, knew something about whales. She believed the dead calves had been underwater for some time and someone was trying to hide their deaths. Disgusted by the killings and upset the carcasses were not made available for study, she encouraged people to contact their state lawmakers about legislation being introduced in January 1971 to protect whales and other marine mammals.[21]

With the finger of suspicion pointing directly at Griffin and Goldsberry, Goldsberry announced that he was "checking into" the deaths and that they might, or might not, have been caused by his operation.[22]

Soon a fourth calf, attached by a line of yellow rope to a seventy-five-pound anchor and with its stomach slit, washed up at Greenbank on Whidbey Island. Using the serial numbers on the anchor, the Island County sheriff contacted marine supply firms to see if it could be linked to an owner, only to be told that it would be difficult to trace an anchor by the number.[23]

How did those calves die? One member of the capture team, Dr. Terrell Newby, offered an answer. Then a young man intent on pursuing a career in marine mammalogy, he first met Griffin in 1965.

Newby was asked to assist and take notes during the capture and joined Griffin and Goldsberry after they had secured their gear and nets in Penn Cove. He rowed around in an eight-foot skiff, crowding the whales so that the calves could be separated from the mothers. Although the animals were guarded constantly, two Coupeville men, Ron Bertsch and Michael Park, paddled out in a small boat under cover of darkness. Moving between the whales milling outside the nets, they cut a large hole in the nets with a bread knife. Ron Bertsch thinks that one female swam free.[24]

An anchor used to sink a dead baby whale in Penn Cove, at home of Joe Beckley, Coupeville. *Author collection.*

Crowding whales, 1970 Penn Cove capture. *Wallie V. Funk Photographs, Center for Pacific Northwest Studies, Western Libraries Heritage Resources, Western Washington University–Bellingham.*

To this day, Newby believes the environmentalists' well-meaning actions had caused the calves to become trapped in the nets and drown. He recalls a heated argument between Griffin and Goldsberry at the Captain Whidbey Inn, where the capture team was staying, about the disposal of the carcasses. Both Griffin and Newby advocated admitting the losses and letting the carcasses go for research. Knowing how public feeling was already stirred up against them, Goldsberry disagreed. Together, he and Newby drove to Seattle in a Fiat sportster to buy chains and anchors. Crowe, the diver who had broken down when Lolita was taken away, assisted with the covert operation to dispose of the carcasses. It was an action that would weigh heavily on his conscience and one that would ultimately play an important part toward the protection of killer whales in Washington State.

Newby recalls that he and biologist Allen Wolman, from the Fish and Wildlife Service's Marine Mammal Laboratory in Seattle, recovered one or two of the washed up carcasses in a station wagon and took them to Sand Point Naval Air Station for necropsy. "The stench," he says, "would have made a maggot gag."[25]

As the days grew shorter and fall merged into winter, the Southern Residents, mourning their devastating losses, took refuge in the more expansive and less easily accessible waters of the Pacific Ocean. Penn Cove, forever tainted by the sorrowful events of that summer, settled into an uneasy peace. Not surprisingly, the Penn Cove capture, which had been covered by statewide television stations and nationwide news services, was heralded by the *Whidbey News-Times* as the top story of the year.

CHAPTER 7

FAR AND WIDE

The first of the captured Penn Cove whales to leave the Seattle Marine Aquarium was Lil Nooka. On August 19, the thirteen-foot male was flown to Houston International Airport for delivery to Sea-Arama Marineworld in Galveston, Texas.[1]

Cradled in a canvas sling lined with wool blankets, Lil Nooka was accompanied by a Texas A&M (Agricultural and Mechanical) University veterinarian on the journey. The young whale was fed seventy-five pounds of mullet, injected with water to replace lost body fluid and sprayed with salt water to avoid dehydration. Drugs and sedatives were injected to offset potential infection and shock.

On arrival at Sea-Arama, Lil Nooka joined a fellow Southern Resident, Mamuk (captured in 1968). In accordance with the usual practice of familiarizing a whale with its new environment, Lil Nooka was "walked" around the perimeter of the saltwater tank by aquarium employees. Soon he, too, would be trained to perform tricks and entertain the public up to five times a day, just like Mamuk. But Lil Nooka's time at Marineworld and rise to stardom was short-lived; he died in March 1971, seven months after capture.

In early September, two more whales—Chappy,[2] an eleven-foot female, and Jumbo,[3] a fifteen-foot male (the largest of the whales captured)—left Seattle bound for Japan. They were the first killer whales to be purchased by the newly opened "marine mammals' paradise" at Kamogawa SeaWorld in Chiba Prefecture, Japan. There, the two performed within sight and sound of their natural world, the Pacific Ocean, until they died within three months of each other: Chappy in April 1974 of periostitis (inflammation) of the lumbar bone and Jumbo in July 1974 of liver dysfunction.

Clovis, an eleven-foot male,[4] was next to leave the Seattle Marine Aquarium joining Calypso (a previously mentioned A5 Northern Resident captured in December 1969) at Marineland in Antibes, France, also founded in 1970. The two whales were not together for long. Calypso died in December, leaving Clovis alone until his death from clostridial myositis (inflammation of muscle tissue) in February 1973.

Ramu III (later renamed Winston),[5] a thirteen-foot male, made the transatlantic flight to foreign shores for delivery to Windsor Safari Park in Berkshire, England (renamed Legoland in 1996), founded by Billy Smart of Billy Smart's Circus in 1969 and officially opened by Princess Margaret in 1970. One of the park's principal attractions was "Seaworld," where Ramu and five bottlenose dolphins performed several times a day for the paying public. Of the five dolphins, three were male (Smartie, Snappy and Cookie) and two female (Lulu and Honey). Cookie, who was a bit of a bully, had an unusual relationship with Ramu. While waiting in the holding pen before shows, Ramu would press his rostrum against the bars and allow Cookie to bite him.[6]

For the most part, Ramu and the dolphins got on well. He built up a protective relationship with the females, especially Lulu. When marine mammals are forced to live in unnatural conditions and exposed to a dysfunctional social structure created by mixing different species and culturally distinct animals together, antagonistic behavior can develop. At worst, this may be directed toward humans, as has been exhibited in the numerous cases of killer whales attacking trainers. In other scenarios, which can be equally damaging, whales and dolphins in captivity fight, often causing significant injury to one another. Ramu intervened in fights involving Lulu by keeping the other dolphins at bay with his intimidating presence and letting the two females into the holding pen before pushing shut the gate.

Ramu knew how to stop the show. The female dolphins were first "on stage," followed by the males. Ramu, the main attraction and star of the show, was last to make an entrance. As if on cue, once he entered the show pool and began his performance, the dolphins emitted a high-pitched call from their pen. Ramu responded by swimming over to them, screeching and spraying water over the bars of the pen. Despite their efforts to intervene, the trainers were powerless to prevent Ramu from visiting his companions, and the show was brought to an abrupt halt.

Boredom for most captive animals is inevitable, especially those as highly intelligent as orcas, whose natural environment is the ocean with no constricting parameters. Ramu relieved his frustration by pushing and bending the steel bars of the dolphin pen. Another way of alleviating his boredom was to fill his mouth with water to spray people. The trainers managed to cure him of this habit by walking away with his food. Even so, this did not break the spraying trick entirely. Watching through a window, Ramu would open his mouth, close his eyes and poke out his tongue before spraying a mouthful of water over members of the public and swimming away.

Soon Ramu's increasing size began to affect his performance in the restricted pool space. His large bulk was unable to gain sufficient angle to reenter the water cleanly, and he began to show signs of aggression. Trainer Doug Cartlidge, who worked with both Cuddles and Ramu, states:[7]

Ramu was the first orca I worked with that was "raw." His only other trainer had left shortly after Ramu arrived at Windsor because of the reputation of Cuddles...I initially trained the head in mouth and then the ride...which at that time were spectacular tricks. He would, at times, close slowly and gently while I had my head in his mouth, causing slight indentations but no real problems. After about three years, we started to see aggression, normally after a trick had not been done properly and a negative signal was given. One thing I saw every time was what we called "red eye" [sign of anger], where the white of his eyes would go bright red for the duration of the incident. Their Royal Highnesses Prince Charles and Prince Andrew did swim with him and he started showing signs of aggression, so they were removed before it developed and knew nothing about it.

In 1974, I survived an attack by Ramu in the water during a show. I received leg injuries and stitches, but know that I was very lucky to live through it. I continued to work with him for some months, but as the management didn't show any concerns or fulfill promises to improve the pool size, which they had been making for years, I left for Sea World, Australia.

As well as royalty, other well-known celebrities came to see Ramu, including the Shah of Iran, pop-singer Rod Stewart and film stars Peter Sellers and Sean Connery.[8]

In 1975, Windsor Safari Park entered into negotiations with SeaWorld San Diego, and on October 17, 1976, Ramu set off on yet another journey across the Atlantic Ocean. It was not a smooth one.

In order to take his measurements in preparation for the arduous trip, Ramu was beached. After a watertight gate was fitted, the pool was drained. Ramu's transport crate, built in San Diego, arrived at the park in August 1976 and was put into storage, where it remained until three days before the scheduled journey. Ramu had been measured for the crate in 1975. When the crate was removed from storage, it was quite obvious that there was no way he would fit into it.

Again Ramu was beached while measurements were taken—he had grown more than four inches wider and a foot and seven inches longer, measuring just over four feet wide and nineteen feet long. With the help of Goldsberry and SeaWorld veterinarian Lanny Cornell, the park's maintenance team fitted an extension tail-guard and re-welded the fiberglass crate to accommodate Ramu's increased girth.

To prevent defecation and sickness on the long journey, Ramu's food intake was reduced. Two days before leaving British soil, he was fed fifty-nine pounds of fish; on the day of departure, he ate nothing.

Blood samples had been taken in the week prior to departure to ensure that Ramu had a clean bill of health. With the problem of the crate resolved, health checks complete and papers signed, Ramu was ready to leave Windsor Safari Park, his home for the past six years. It was time to say farewell to his dolphin friends, who, with the added disruption of press and television crews earlier in the day, were totally confused.

With Ramu contained in the holding pen, a driver was sent to collect the crate. When the truck carrying the crate arrived, the driver accidentally drove over a steel fence post, tearing a brake cylinder. An urgent message for assistance was sent to Heathrow Airport and another truck dispatched. Meanwhile, the park's maintenance crew carried out emergency repairs. Once these were completed, everything was in place. Or so it seemed, until a message arrived announcing that the plane had been held up in Belgium.

There was a further two-hour delay. Once the water level in the holding pen had been lowered to waist height, Ramu was beached yet again. The water level was then raised so he could be maneuvered onto a stretcher. With seven wet-suited men alongside him in the pool, the nine-thousand-pound Ramu was manhandled on to the supporting canvas stretcher. But with one quick flick of his powerful tail flukes, he slid off, and the whole process began all over again.

Before lifting Ramu from the pool, handlers checked the sling to ensure that stretcher burns were avoided, if possible. Once Ramu was hoisted by crane and lowered onto the truck, he was dried off with towels and given a coating of cod-liver ointment to protect his skin. After further transition to a foam rubber–lined crate, ice was packed around his enormous body.

Following customs clearance at London's Heathrow Airport, Ramu was ready for takeoff. The original crate had been made to specifications to fit through the cargo door of the plane, a Flying Tigers Stretch DC-8. Since then, a number of changes had been made. However, no one took this into consideration when making the travel arrangements, and the crate would not pass into the hold. There was now no alternative but to remove the tailboard and physically turn Ramu's tail around to enter the plane. Nobody relished the task, as Ramu had never liked having his tail touched. Fortunately for the transport team, and despite considerable vocalization, Ramu did not, on this occasion, react. After some further pushing and shoving, he was safely contained in the cargo hold. All that now remained was for the fire brigade to half-fill the crate with fresh water before more ice and spraying equipment were packed in.

At 1:15 p.m., the plane taking Ramu to San Diego taxied onto the runway. Rumbling along the tarmac as it gathered momentum, the plane was soon airborne, and Ramu was destined for the same shores he had left six years earlier. The clunk of the landing gear locking into place ready for touch down nine or ten hours later heralded the plane's arrival at Lindbergh Field, San Diego. Two forklifts shunted across the runway to await Ramu's exit from the cargo hold before depositing him on to a flatbed truck for the fifteen-minute ride to SeaWorld.

After eighteen hours out of the water, during which he was beached three times, hoisted by crane and forklift, manhandled, contained in a crate and exposed to differing levels of unfamiliar noises and alien sensations both on the ground and in the air, Ramu arrived at SeaWorld San Diego. He was, once again, in proximity to the Pacific Ocean, where his life began and, for all intents and purposes, ended. SeaWorld renamed him Winston, and as at Windsor Safari Park, he would share pool space with dolphins. Now, though, he would perform under the stage name "Shamu."

Winston's move to San Diego may have been an exchange deal between SeaWorld and Windsor Safari Park for three dolphins and, a year later, two female orcas named Hoi Wai and Winnie (captured in Iceland in 1977 and kept at the Dolfinarium Harderwijk, Netherlands, before being purchased by SeaWorld).[9] Winnie (formerly called Frya) was named after the wife of the park's manager. She achieved certain notoriety as the last orca kept in captivity in Britain, following an overhaul by the Department of the Environment in 1985 of the standards and requirements for keeping killer whales in marine parks.

Biologists Dr. Susan Brown and Dr. Margaret Klinowska had reviewed the marine parks' existing conditions and standards and put forward suggestions for ways to improve the facilities.[10] Although their report was critical of the marine parks, it still failed to satisfy environmental groups who felt the recommendations did not go far enough. A steering committee was set up by the Department of the Environment (now part of the Department of the Environment, Food and Rural Affairs) to consider comments from both the environmental groups and the marine park industry and to review the recommendations already made. Five years later, in 1990, the secretary of state for the Department of the Environment published a revised report containing a list of guidelines, including minimum pool size, water quality and handling of animals. The minimum amount of water for the main pool containing up to five orcas should be 3.2 million gallons with an average depth of forty-nine feet and minimum depth of thirty-nine feet. Even though these standards are the strictest in the world, they were still below the recommendations made in the draft report.

Another critical guideline was introduced, which banned the keeping of solitary animals. Winnie had been kept at Windsor Safari Park on her own for a number of years. Faced with its inability to finance and meet the 1993 deadline to upgrade and comply with the new standards, the park abandoned the struggle. Like Ramu III (Winston), Winnie made the transatlantic crossing in October 1991.[11] Her destination was SeaWorld Florida on "breeding loan" until 1994, when she was moved to SeaWorld Ohio. Five years later, she was transferred yet again to SeaWorld San Antonio and died in April 2002 from a blocked intestine. According to the marine park, pieces of a broken ceramic tile, coins and other objects ingested during her time at the Windsor Safari Park contributed to her death.

During his time at SeaWorld, Winston impregnated various females, including Kandu V, Kenau and Katina. Of the three mothers, Katina was the first to give birth to a healthy young female, Kalina, the first of the "Baby Shamu" whale calves. Neither Kandu V nor Kenau was so lucky—Kandu V's calf was stillborn, and Kenau's calf died from a heart defect eleven days after she was born.

Winston, with his dorsal fin flopped over on one side, remained at SeaWorld until his death in April 1986 from chronic cardiovascular failure.

In October 1970, Ramu IV, an eleven-and-a-half-foot male, followed in his namesake's footsteps (Ramu II) to Marineland of Australia, flying first to San Francisco and then by cargo jet on the inaugural Quantas service to Sydney.[12] For a short time, Ramu IV was to enjoy the dubious distinction of being the only killer whale in captivity in the southern hemisphere. Sadly, like his predecessor captured in 1969 and who died in 1970, Ramu IV died a year after being taken into captivity.

The last of the captured calves torn from her mother in Penn Cove was taken to the Miami Seaquarium, Florida, where she arrived on September 24, 1970. Her name is Lolita, although before that she was called Tokitae, a Coast Salish greeting meaning "nice day" or "pretty colors." The late Dr. Jesse White (1935–1995), a marine mammal veterinarian, went to the Seattle Marine Aquarium to select a suitable whale for public display at the Seaquarium.[13] According to White's daughter, Lisa, he saw something special in the little whale and chose a name that would reflect her courage, beauty and gentleness. Her name was later changed to Lolita, a better fit for the glitzy Miami image and to deflect awkward questions about Tokitae's true background and place of origin. She is the only surviving Southern Resident orca still in captivity from the capture era (the rest had died by 1987) and remains at her original place of transfer, the Miami Seaquarium, opened in 1955. Owned by Arthur Hertz and his son, Andrew, of Wometco Enterprises Inc. (although it was announced on March 28, 2014, that a sale to California-based Palace Entertainments has been agreed), it is the longest operating oceanarium in the United States. Lolita performs for forty-five minutes twice a day, every day, for the paying public, with only dolphins for company since her companion, Hugo (captured 1968), died in 1980.

At the time of capture, Lolita was recorded as being about fourteen feet long and aged four to six years old. Her home today is a seventy-three-foot-wide, eighty-foot-long pool, which doubles as a performance pool and holding area. The pool is the smallest killer whale tank in the United States and is considered to be in violation of the Animal Welfare Act (AWA). Both the AWA and the Animal and Plant Health Inspection Service (APHIS) state that, for a whale of Lolita's size, the main enclosure should be forty-eight feet wide in either direction, with a straight line of travel across the middle. Lolita's tank is thirty-five feet from the front wall to the slide-out barrier and, at its deepest central point, twenty feet deep. In December 1995, the United States Department of Agriculture (USDA) carried out an investigation in response to the Humane Society of the United States filing a formal complaint claiming that the twenty-

Lolita at the Miami Seaquarium. *Photo by Ken Balcomb, Center for Whale Research.*

Lolita with her only orca companion. *Photo by Howard Garrett.*

five-year-old tank did not meet the minimum size regulations. Even before this date, a USDA inspector cast doubts on whether the pool's size complied with the required standards.[14]

The big issue with Lolita's tank is the way in which the pool is measured. Should the concrete island in the middle of the perfume bottle–shaped pool be included in the diameter measurements? The Miami Seaquarium claims it should. If that section is included, the diameter is sixty feet, thus exceeding the legal requirements. If it is excluded, the horizontal dimension from the front wall to the wall forming the barrier/work station island is only thirty-five feet, thirteen feet less than the minimum legal requirements of at least forty-eight feet in both directions. APHIS claims that the workstation, where Lolita rests during the show, is a floating formation. It is, in fact, a solid concrete structure—she cannot get underneath it and, with gates on both ends, does not have free movement. Another bone of contention is that Lolita has no protection from the weather, including hurricanes, or shade from the hot Miami sun. Her skin is treated with zinc oxide (just like Namu during his journey to Seattle), stained black to help protect her from sunburn.

APHIS turned a blind eye to the complaint filed by the Humane Society of the United States (HSUS) and as recently as August 2010 stated that there were "no non-compliant items found" during its inspection of the Seaquarium.

As for the Seaquarium's promise to build a new, larger tank for Lolita (which it has been promising since 1978), so far nothing has been done to replace the dilapidated pool, which in places is held together by industrial jacks. In November 1999, well over a decade ago, Arthur Hertz appeared on Miami television saying that construction of Lolita's new tank would begin "in six months."

Over forty years of Lolita's life has been spent in a tiny tank serving the public in the name of "entertainment," putting millions of dollars into the pockets of her owners. Her time in captivity is surpassed only by that of Corky II, a Northern Resident captured in December 1969 in Pedder Bay, British Columbia, and still performing as "Shamu" at SeaWorld San Diego.

A female orca named "Whale" was the last of the Southern Residents to be captured in 1970, when she stranded at Port Madison, Bainbridge Island. The eight-hundred-pound calf was spotted on the morning of Thursday, August 6. When the whales were being pursued toward the south end of Whidbey Island, some may have slipped away farther south at Possession Sound. The little whale may have become separated from a pod reported in Miller's Bay on Bainbridge Island or quite simply may have become a straggling victim of the hunt, unable to keep up with the rest of her family. Another orca chased into Miller's Bay the previous weekend managed to escape before divers from the Seattle Marine Aquarium crew could corral the fleeing animal. One lost whale did not seem to worry Griffin's operation too much. A representative from the aquarium commented, "They're coming in from the ocean by the hundreds—nobody knows why."[15]

The aquarium was not quite so philosophical about letting Whale get away. Two divers from the Seattle Marine Aquarium tried unsuccessfully to catch her and, with darkness falling, gave up the chase. They found her the next day and drove her onto the beach. Griffin, arriving by seaplane, supervised the "rescue" on the grounds that she was a nursing calf

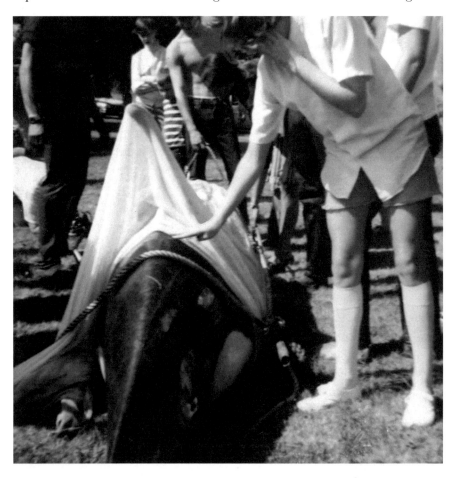

"Whale," a casualty of the hunt at Bainbridge Island. *Photo by Joan Bickerton, courtesy of Connie Bickerton.*

and would not survive on her own. With the help of the neighborhood community, Whale was hoisted onto a truck and driven away to the Seattle Marine Aquarium, her chance of freedom gone forever. Griffin's efforts and justification for the capture did not gain favor with everyone; a number of local residents made it clear they would have much preferred to see Whale chased back out to sea.

Although the original plan was for Whale (or Wally, as she became known) to stay at the Seattle Marine Aquarium for display, replacing Kandu I, Whale was sold and flown to the Munich Aquarium in Germany a month later. There she performed ten to twelve shows daily and became a side attraction for the annual Oktoberfest. She reportedly died of a heart attack after becoming ill in October 1971, a year after being orphaned and captured.[16]

In the same year that the Southern Residents lost another eight members of their community to the entertainment industry and more died in the capture process, SeaWorld opened its second park in Aurora, Ohio.

In the meantime, while the insidious depletion of the Southern Resident population continued, the U.S. Department of the Interior placed eight other species of whale (fin, sei, sperm, bowhead, blue, humpback, gray and North Pacific right whale) on the endangered list

Display of commercial products manufactured from whale parts. *Courtesy Uko Gorter.*

under the Endangered Species Conservation Act of 1970, the precursor to the current Endangered Species Act. Import of whale products, used largely for cat food but also as an oil base for margarine, soap and cream, was also banned in the United States.[17]

While it was conceded that little study had been done on killer whales, they were not considered a threatened species. The consensus of opinion was that they were the more numerous of the whales spread across the globe, with many inhabiting the waters of Puget Sound. Although some contact had been made with Canadian researchers to conduct a census, no definite plans had been made. Because the federally funded Sand Point Naval Air Station, the only whale research center in Washington State, was moving to La Jolla, California, any future killer whale studies were unlikely to be undertaken.[18]

CHAPTER 8

THE HUNTERS RETURN

ollowing public pressure and the outcry occasioned by the Penn
Cove captures, the U.S. House Committee on Natural Resources
met in January 1971 and voted in favor of giving the state Game
Commission the authority to regulate the hunting and capture of killer
whales. A few months later, in early August, the Washington State
legislature passed a law regulating future captures by requiring a permit
and payment of $1,000 per whale. The presence of officials from the
Department of Game to ensure humane handling and prevent harassment
was also required.[1]

Prior to the Department of Game's assuming authority over the
management of marine mammals, Griffin and Goldsberry's company,
Namu Inc., applied to that department for a permit to capture six killer
whales.[2] Following a public hearing, the request was granted. The permit
issued on August 20, 1971, authorized Namu Inc. to capture and remove six
killer whales from the wild subject to certain conditions:[3]

1. *Whales can be captured or corralled only in nets, and there shall be no
   purse rings or purse lines on said nets. In addition, they can be taken
   where naturally or accidentally stranded.*
2. *No animal shall be taken smaller than 8 feet total length, or larger than
   16 feet total length.*
3. *The permittee must have available an adequate marine aquarium tank in
   which to condition and hold whales taken, which has been approved by*

the Department of Game. He shall also have the services of a competent marine mammal veterinarian.

4. The Game Department, Game Management Division, in Olympia, or a Regional Supervisor, shall be notified promptly when any whales are being held in a net or nets.

5. Animals contained in nets shall be surveyed and sorted promptly without undue delay, and no animals shall be confined in nets for more than ten (10) days.

6. Within five (5) days after taking a killer whale, the permittee shall pay to the Game Department the sum of $1,000.00 as the fee for taking such whales prescribed by law.

7. This permit is valid from the date of issuance to March 31, 1972.

8. The Director of Game reserves the right to cancel this permit at any time for cause or for violations of these provisions in addition to any criminal penalties prescribed by law.

A Washington State Department of Game report headed "Killer Whale Management" set out the procedure used to capture killer whales:[4]

The permittee operating in Washington waters presently has at his disposal a small float plane used for spotting whales, and a small, fast sixteen-foot outboard boat for herding, and a 32-foot fiberglass gill net boat powered by twin engines of 475 horsepower for setting the nylon capture net and transporting the whales to their base of operations.

When the whales have been spotted, the small outboard and the gill net boat work as a team, herding the pod to an area that is sheltered and with a good bottom to set the capture net, which has a seven-and-one-half inch mesh and is half a mile long. After the whales are in the desired area, the outboard boat towing the net encircles the pod.

The floatplane returns to the base of operations as soon as the pod is captured and returns with scuba divers, who are then at the capture area on a 24-hour schedule.

The divers immediately inspect the net around the perimeter, both inside and outside, and set the 75-pound anchors to shape the net and hold it in place.

Floating docks mounted on Styrofoam logs are towed to the capture area and joined together to form a U-shaped structure six feet wide and 80 feet to the side. This forms the actual capture pen and provides a working area during the operation.

The time consumed during these phases of the operation involves about two days, which allows the whales to acclimate to their new surroundings.

During this initial period, they utilize echolocation for determining the boundaries to which they are confined. After they have settled down, they rely on visual senses when moving around the area and are seen constantly rising up, or eyeballing.

Their behavior is similar to other herd-type mammals, where the female takes the initiative and leads the pod, with the bulls following.

During their confinement, a series of tail and pectoral fin slapping on the surface of the water triggers an impressive aerial display of whales leaping full length out of the water for a period of several minutes. This is repeated periodically throughout the day.

An observer cannot help but be impressed with the knowledge these mammals possess and that their confinement could be short-lived with a sudden charge through or over the net floats.

Upon completion of the dock installation and adjacent catch pen, a smaller seine net is used to sort the whales into a smaller group and herd these into the catch pen where the actual selection of the whales to be taken occurs.

The gate, or drop net at the entrance to the catch pen, is secured when the whales move voluntarily into this area.

A platform mounted on the sixteen-foot boat at the bottom of the U-serves as the platform for putting the noose over the whale that is selected. The hoop for putting the noose on is split at the top to form a split circle, and the line, a soft woven nylon, is held to the loop by thread or rubber bands. When the noose goes past the pectoral fins, the crew on the dock tighten up the main line and haul the selected whale to the dock, where he is supported by lines and padding under the head and tail. As soon as these supporting lines are in place, the whale becomes submissive and rests there.

At this time, all measurements are taken from the whale and recorded. The whale is inspected by a marine mammal veterinarian, and antibiotic injections are administered. The divers then place a canvas cradle with holes for the pectoral fins under the whale, which supports the major length of the whale. The large block and tackle on the 32-foot boat raises the supported whale onto the stern of the boat, where it is covered and kept moist for the short trip back to the aquarium.

While Namu Inc.'s permit was being processed, in response to the public controversy over the capture of killer whales, a young marine

A Tribute to the late Dr. Michael Bigg, PhD (1939-1990)
"The Father of Killer Whale Research"

Tribute to Dr. Michael Bigg at Telegraph Cove, British Columbia. *Author collection.*

biologist, Dr. Michael A. Bigg (1939–1990) from the Fisheries Research Board of Canada Biological Station, Nanaimo, British Columbia, was asked by the Canadian Ministry of the Environment to conduct a study off Vancouver Island to assess the number of killer whales. Bigg, whose doctorate was in the study of harbor seals, took on the project with enthusiasm.[5]

Well over sixteen thousand questionnaires were sent out by Bigg's research team, which included biologists Ian B. MacAskie and Graeme Ellis, to boaters, lighthouse keepers, fishermen and other people along the British Columbia coast asking them to watch for, and report, sightings of killer whales on a single day, July 27. Another one thousand questionnaires were distributed in Washington State; others were distributed in Alaska, California and Oregon.

The information requested was fairly basic: the number of whales seen, including mature males and calves; time of sightings; and direction of travel. Out of the 16,500 questionnaires, 538 were completed and returned. To help establish data, duplicate sightings of the same group of killer whales were determined by assuming that each group did not change markedly on that date and traveled no faster than seven knots per hour.

Although adverse weather conditions of rain and fog affected the exercise, 60 percent of killer whales were sighted in two areas—southeast Vancouver Island and northeast Vancouver Island (Johnstone Strait). Whether the distribution reflected a larger number of killer whales in the two regions than in others or whether the fact that 65 percent of the observers were located there was unknown. The 538 observers spent 4,918 hours watching whales and reported 549 sightings: British Columbia (360); Washington (114); Oregon (0); California (13)—observed July 24, 1971; Alaska (62).

The results gave cause for concern. Up until now, it had been assumed that there were hundreds of killer whales, even thousands. It emerged from this one-day census that there were fewer than originally thought.

Far from being intimidated by their increasing unpopularity, on August 21, 1971, the day after the permit to Namu Inc. was granted and almost a year to the day after the devastating 1970 Penn Cove capture, Griffin and Goldsberry returned to the scene of the crime—except that in the eyes of the law, none had been committed. They assured the Department of Game that the helicopter at their disposal was for observing whales in the nets.[6]

Unlike the previous year, when they drove the Southern Resident community into Penn Cove, Griffin and Goldsberry were not quite so lucky on this occasion. Even so, they were still successful in capturing fifteen to twenty-four whales.[7] With new legislation in force, their activities were overseen by the Department of Game, which was now responsible for the management of marine mammals.

Not only was the Department of Game present, but also KING 5 reporter Don McGaffin was on the scene. A New York native, McGaffin obtained a master's degree in journalism from Columbia University and worked for newspaper companies on the East Coast before moving to

Don McGaffin, KOMO4 and KING5 news reporter. *Courtesy Mimi Sheridan.*

California. After leaving there, he went to work for **KOMO** 4 and **KING** 5 Seattle in the 1970s and 1980s, reporting and producing documentaries. He was passionate about seeing justice done, sadly passing away in 2005 while in the process of writing a book about his life. His memoirs include a powerful account of the 1971 Penn Cove capture.

Like several other Seattle television people in the early '70s keen to get a taste of island life, McGaffin scraped together enough money to buy a place on Whidbey Island. While taking a few days vacation to clean up the former newspaper offices he had sunk his cash into, he spotted the unmistakable sight of shining black-and-white orcas diving and surfacing in Penn Cove.

"They exploded right in front of me," McGaffin wrote, "...leaping breaches, rolling, huffing, water slapping, HUGE fins. It was magnificent... stunning...and solemn."

As he watched the impressive parade breaking through the azure water, McGaffin gave little thought to the seaplane circling high overhead. He was too intent on calling KING 5 News office to ask them to send a reporter and cameraman over to film the magnificent spectacle.

But it was vacation time. Somebody might be there tomorrow, maybe the following day. No promises.

The next morning, KING 5 cameraman Bill Dorsey arrived on McGaffin's doorstep. There was no sign of a reporter. Resigned to losing his vacation time if the story was to be covered, McGaffin set off with Dorsey to find Frank Hennings, the Coupeville harbor master. He needed someone with a boat to ferry him and Dorsey out to photograph such a newsworthy event. Twelve months after the notorious Penn Cove capture, whales had once again been herded into Penn Cove and were trapped in the nets.

Loading their bulky camera equipment into Hennings's small black motorboat, the trio puttered deeper toward a U-shaped floating pier. Hundreds of feet of lines, topped with corks, swung from three sides; mesh nets dangled from the fourth side. Occasionally a glistening dorsal fin, reflecting the sunlight, surfaced behind the lines.

Hennings maneuvered the boat alongside the undulating pier, watched closely by two wet-suited divers, hands resting on hips.

"Ahoy there, gentlemen," McGaffin spoke first. "We're from KING 5 News. Okay if we come aboard?"

The divers turned away.

"All right, all right, come aboard," a stocky, barrel-chested man kneeling nearby, mumbled irritably. "But stay out of the damned way." It was Donald Goldsberry.

Dorsey set to work. He filmed the whales in the pen from every angle, standing, kneeling and squatting on the wooden float. "Jesus, they're big," he murmured as they twisted, dived and turned in search of an escape route.

Suddenly, an eerie noise split the tranquility of the cove.

"I can't describe it," McGaffin wrote. "The breathy whine…the cry…the long, weeping, keening cry…"; then, "we were surrounded by another weird, wonderful sound. The killers outside the nets were calling to the orca trapped in the nets. But there was a human note in that cry, a sobbing mewl."

McGaffin shivered listening to the plaintive, heart-rending cries. The capture team, indifferent to the film crew and the animals' plight, carried on with their work.

Curious about their hostile attitude, McGaffin turned to Reade Brown, one of the officers present from the Department of Game, and asked why the capture team was so "standoffish."

"It's probably because of the killings last year," Brown replied.

"Killings? Who was killed?"

Brown briefly recounted the story of the previous year's captures.

Staring hard at them from a small, semicircular bridge built over the pen, where he had been trying to lasso an agitated whale, stood a slender young man with a mop of brown hair. It was Ted Griffin.

Nothing was going to stop McGaffin from making his report. Gazing directly at the camera, he picked up the microphone: "Soon they will pick the killers that will be sent to California…the State Game Department is on the scene…last year three orcas washed up on the beach near here a month after the whale catchers left. They'd been sunk with rocks in their bellies. But the whale catchers firmly deny knowing anything about it."

The next morning, KING 5 News photographer Jeff Mart arrived at McGaffin's house. He told McGaffin he'd gone out in his own boat and tried to board the floating pier. The capture team stopped him.

"They're really mad at you," he told McGaffin. "That story you did last night. Some of them saw it on the air. Goldsberry said if I got within 50 yards of their pier they'd dump me, my camera and my boat into the cove." He paused to draw breath before adding, "and [they said] if McGaffin came out here, they'd kill him."

McGaffin guffawed and reached for his keys. Nobody was going to threaten him.

With Mart wearing his body pod, an aluminum contraption holding up the heavy Auricon camera, and a belt full of batteries strapped around his waist, McGaffin boarded Frank Hennings's small boat. This time, Hennings had his young son with him.

Motoring toward the U-shaped pier, McGaffin counted five boats stretched out in a line ahead of them. One was a Boston whaler, another a big marine launch. Three medium-sized outboards made up the rest of the fleet.

Suddenly, without warning, the marine launch, engines at full throttle, headed menacingly toward them. The remaining boats followed.

McGaffin recalls, "A vicious wave torn up by the speeding launch smashed into us broadside...another speeding craft charged across our wake as yet another craft hurled another wake at us on the other side. Water cascaded in at us as our boat rocked and twisted in the churning waves. Another boat ripped by us."

Hennings, fearful for his son's life, held on tightly to the boy's belt as the launch circled nearby. The Boston whaler, with Griffin at the helm, closed in behind Hennings's motorboat. Reaching over, Griffin grabbed the outboard's gas line, twisting and pulling it.

"You son of a bitch," McGaffin shouted, lunging forward with a punch. He missed. Griffin sped away, grinning over his shoulder.

The armada wasted no time in initiating another attack. The marine launch, engines roaring, swept past, drenching the party in its wake. Despite the avalanche of water, Mart managed to get a clear shot of Goldsberry.

Fearful that their pursuers might try to steal the damning evidence, McGaffin urged Hennings to drop them off at the dock of the Captain Whidbey Inn. Abandoning the boat, he rushed up the steps, anxious to find the proprietor, Steve Stone. After explaining the urgency, he handed the taped canister over to Stone for safekeeping and phoned KING 5 to arrange for a plane to collect the film as soon as possible.

McGaffin was first and foremost a reporter, and despite the frightening attack, he wanted more footage of the orcas. This time Hennings's son stayed on shore.

Knowing there was no way he would ever be able to board the floating pier, McGaffin asked Reade Brown if they could tie up alongside the Game Department's launch. Brown agreed.

Several divers waited around the pens viewing the whales dispassionately, while women with children watched the capture operation from the Game Department's launch. McGaffin threw Brown a mooring rope.

"Sorry," Brown's hushed voice was almost a whisper, "but I can't let you aboard. He's pretty upset," he jerked his head in Griffin's direction.

"Griffin's upset?" McGaffin snarled. "That son of a bitch Griffin could have drowned one of us this morning. And, he's upset? Come on Reade…"

He was interrupted by a low, breathy voice.

"Hey, McGaffin. Just try to touch this pier, and we'll break you in two," Griffin threatened. Beckoning McGaffin toward him, he murmured, "Come on, we'll turn you inside out and feed your ass to the crabs."

Brown disappeared inside the cabin of the launch. McGaffin shouted after him, "If we can't come aboard, did you ask Griffin if those wives and children could come aboard?" They, too, scuttled out of sight.

There was nothing to do but leave.

As Hennings steered away, Griffin sneered and raised his left hand, middle finger projected.

Enraged by the insult and the Game Department's ineffectual response, McGaffin dwelt on the memory of the small boy without a life vest who could barely swim and who could so easily have drowned; a photographer weighed down by his body suit and camera equipment could have been killed. An incriminating news film could have been lost, and if it had been, few people would believe the story.

But while McGaffin brooded, Mart went into action. As Hennings circled the nets, Mart photographed the captured orcas. The poignant pictures would be shown on KING 5 News that evening along with McGaffin's dramatic coverage of the wild boat chase.

The following night, McGaffin and his wife booked a table for dinner at the Captain Whidbey Inn. Goldsberry sat nearby with some of his crew. Glancing toward the lobby, McGaffin saw half a dozen people waiting to be seated, Griffin among them.

Excusing himself, McGaffin strode through the double doors housing the kitchen and along the hallway to the lobby. Griffin stood by a large wing armchair near the dining-room entrance. McGaffin paused, smiling, in front of him and raised his right forefinger. At the same time, he laid his left hand on his chest. It was a move his father had taught him many years ago. A bemused Griffin followed the protruding finger with inquisitive eyes.

"As you were saying yesterday from the pier…" McGaffin hit his opponent with a left hook, knocking him out cold as he fell backward into the chair.

Fearing repercussions, McGaffin hastily returned to the dining room. No one seemed to have noticed anything—except his wife.

"Are you all right?" she asked. "You look, well, funny."

Conscious of his shaking hands and beads of perspiration on his face, McGaffin said he'd had to run back to the car. Goldsberry looked across at the couple, grinning insolently. McGaffin urged his wife to hurry. Griffin would soon regain consciousness, and it wouldn't be long before Island County sheriff's deputies were on their way.

But the deputies never came. McGaffin could only conclude that the tall, macho athletic young diver didn't want it made public that a forty-year-old, five foot nine, 158-pounder had flattened him with just one punch—and a left at that. He never saw Griffin again.[8]

McGaffin's harrowing documentation of the Penn Cove capture almost disappeared. A rusting canister containing the film was found in the archives of KING television many years later.

For the second year running, John Stone witnessed whales in the nets in Penn Cove. Stone, who had moved to another property in the cove after the 1970 capture, recalls his cat trying to hide under the furniture to escape the cries of the whales. He remembers, too, Griffin phoning around various marine parks from the Captain Whidbey Inn, negotiating prices.

Although only three of the whales captured in the latest Penn Cove hunt were kept under the permit, before her release back to the wild, one eighteen-foot, five-inch female was freeze-branded on the left side with the figure "—1" and the letters "U.S." on the dorsal fin.[9] The freeze-branding method, also known as cryo-branding, was developed by Dr. R. Keith Farrell at Washington State University in 1966 and provides permanent identification. Cold branding irons are chilled using a mixture of alcohol and dry ice or liquid nitrogen; this method is considered to be less painful and damaging than hot branding.

The three whales—Kona, Kandu II and Kandu III—believed to be from L pod, were transferred to the Seattle Marine Aquarium and held there for a month before being transported to their future homes.

The two females, Kona and Kandu III, were sent to SeaWorld San Diego. Kona spent one season performing at SeaWorld Aurora. She died of septicemia at age twelve, too young at that time to be involved in any breeding program.

Kandu III performed along with Kona and was one of the original orcas to perform at SeaWorld Orlando when the park opened in December 1973. She died from *Uraemia-Nephritis* (kidney failure) in June 1975.

Kandu II, the male, made the transatlantic flight to Bremen, West Germany, where the annual Oktoberfest celebration was underway.[10] Accompanied by Goldsberry, Kandu II was flown by Air Canada back across the Atlantic to Toronto before being loaded onto a truck bound for his new home, Marineland and Game Farm in Niagara Falls (now known as Marineland of Canada Inc.), where he performed until his death from pneumonia in 1979. He was the first orca on display at the amusement park and the star attraction. Later, he shared the limelight briefly with Kandy, a female member of L pod captured in Pedder Bay, British Columbia, in August 1973. When Kandy died three months after her arrival, Kandu II was on his own until he was joined by Knootka (Nootka), a Transient captured in March 1970 in Pedder Bay, and Kanduke, another Transient captured in August 1975 in Pedder Bay. He continued to perform at Marineland until his death from pneumonia in 1979.

In 2001, Canadian MP Libby Davies tabled a private member's bill (a bill introduced in the House of Commons by a member of parliament who is not a cabinet minister) in an attempt to ban the capture and trade in live dolphins and whales following a number of cetacean deaths at Marineland of Canada Inc.[11] She was unsuccessful. Following a scientific study by Department of Fisheries and Oceans, then minister for fisheries and oceans Herb Dhaliwal failed to act on the recommendations. "Kandu's Twister," a teacup-style ride featuring orcas painted on the sides of large swiveling "teacups," was introduced at Marineland in 2002 and continues to delight thrill-seekers to this day.

On August 29, a few days after the latest Penn Cove capture, the original Shamu, star of the "Shamu Goes Hollywood" show and the first Southern Resident to be captured in 1965, died of an infection.[12] But even though her disturbed and turbulent history might disappear in the annals of time, Shamu would embrace immortality in the trademark name. A naïve and trusting public was unlikely to be able to tell the difference between one performing orca and another.

Coupeville Whale Wheel, designed by Tsimshian artist Roger Purdue to honor the orcas captured and killed in the Penn Cove captures. *Author collection.*

The Penn Cove roundup was not the only capture in 1971. In November, under the permit granted on August 20, 1971, Griffin and Goldsberry captured nineteen whales in Carr Inlet, Washington State. Two young males, official designations SEQ-OO-C7104 and SEQ-OO-C7105, were taken to the Seattle Marine Aquarium.[13] Neither survived, but each still counted under the permit. Griffin and Goldsberry were now one short of their allotted number of six.

With the permit due to expire on March 31, 1972, Namu Inc. had to move fast. Scouting the waters of Puget Sound with added intensity, the hunters were successful in locating, and capturing, eleven whales at Purdy, Tacoma, in March 1972. It was unfortunate for the one young whale selected, Canuck, that he was deprived of his freedom so close to the date of the expiration of the permit.

A study of the Southern Residents undertaken years later found that, based on association, Canuck has an impressive lineage. His official designation was J24.[14] He is believed to be the son of Sissy (J12), whose mother, Granny (J2), is the oldest matriarch of the Southern Resident community. His uncle was the iconic Ruffles (J1), who would be indelibly imprinted on John Stone's memory. Canuck's sister, Samish (J14), born in 1974, was one of the first calves to be documented from birth by Canadian researcher Mike Bigg.

But Canuck never knew his sister, Samish, or her family. His destination was to be SeaWorld San Diego, where he was transferred in April 1972.

Canuck did not spend long in captivity. He died in December 1974 of candidiasis (a fungal infection) at SeaWorld Orlando.[15]

In a summing up of their first year of killer whale management, the Department of Game concluded that it had been a successful one, saying, "The whale has been elevated to a status that it rightly deserves, estimated populations have been established, and with the marking of additional whales, knowledge will be obtainable on their movements. Emphasis will be placed on obtaining sex ratio and calf/cow ratio to establish parameters on which to base future management decisions, and permit restrictions will be adjusted to provide adequate protection for this magnificent animal of Washington waters."[16]

CHAPTER 9
CONFLICTS OF INTEREST

After the expiration of its permit, Namu Inc. wasted no time in applying for another one to capture more killer whales. But by now, the public's antipathy toward the burgeoning captive killer whale industry was even stronger. On April 11, 1972, in response to a barrage of complaints from the public, the Game Commission held a public meeting.[1]

Opening the proceedings on behalf of the Department of Game, Chairman Arthur Coffin said the purpose of the hearing was to discuss requests for killer whale capture permits for 1972. Namu Inc. was applying for nine permits; Peter Babich, skipper of the *Pacific Maid*, was applying for three.

In summary, considerable publicity during the prior year had generated some 450 letters in opposition to the practice of capturing killer whales and only 4 or 5 in favor. Most of the letters objected to: taking wild animals and placing them in captivity, the methods used to achieve this and where the captures had taken place.

Records showed that to date, Namu Inc. had captured 192 whales, of which 33 were kept and 9 died during capture.

Claude Bekins, one of the members of the Game Commission, commented that most of the captures had taken place in southern Puget Sound and asked if there was a danger of taking too many whales from a single pod.

Goldsberry assured him that they were selective in their choices, including not taking pregnant females, as "we do have a deep feeling for these animals." He added that if he and Griffin believed they were in any way endangering the species, they would leave the business.

When asked where the whales went when sold, Goldsberry replied that their destinies were mostly oceanariums, adding, "SeaWorld is one of our biggest customers."

The commission raised the issue of the manner in which the whales were captured, which was the subject of many of the complaints. Goldsberry admitted to using harpoons in the early days and containing the animals in wire nets. This method was discontinued after some had drowned. Goldsberry was confident that they had made progress in their capture methods and were learning how to restrain the whales without hurting them.

When asked why he wanted the permits, Goldsberry replied, "Strictly for our knowledge and for the animals to go to oceanariums."

"What are you taking for scientific purposes and what for profit?" one commission member pursued.

"The way I feel about the killer whale, I like them very much. They are an animal that I love, but I am out there to make a dollar," Goldsberry admitted.

When asked if he thought any losses should be charged against his quota after permits were issued, Goldsberry said he didn't care one way or the other. But when pressed by the commission about his thoughts on paying for a permit before finding and trapping whales, he stated emphatically that in that event, Namu Inc. would need to be "a little more intense" in their operations.

The Game Department recognized the strength of public feeling about captures in the southern part of Puget Sound and considered the possibility of limiting permits to the northern area, which would include taking whales around the San Juan Islands. Goldsberry dismissed this suggestion as the whales spent much of their time there in the summer months, which was when most tourists chose to visit the islands.

Neither did Goldsberry want to be restricted to the north of Whidbey Island. He was keen to have another year "inside Whidbey Island to the lower Puget Sound…a prime hunting area of whales which we hate to give up," with "laser beam marking tried on entire pods of whales in order to see where they go." He also wanted to bring an animal to the Seattle Marine Aquarium so that different marking methods could be tried and more learned about migration patterns and population numbers. So far two animals had been marked but were never seen again.

In his capacity as consulting veterinarian for Namu Inc., Dr. Tag Gornall supported keeping captive whales for research purposes. Addressing one of the public's complaints about the use of aircraft to shoot at the whales with ammunition, tranquilizers or sedatives, he told the commission that he had

Southern Resident orcas pass Mount Baker southbound in Admiralty Inlet on the "Chum (salmon) run." *Author collection.*

talked to Goldsberry and "stipulated that the planes will be held off 200 feet above the water to eliminate any harassment of these animals."

Members of the public representing the Tahoma Audubon Society, the Wildlife Committee of the Washington Environmental Council, Friends of the Earth, the American Association of University Women and a number of individuals all opposed the captures.

One person not afraid to speak out was Tacoma resident Dr. Henning, who described himself as "an objective observer." He had seen whales netted in front of his home and witnessed their "extreme agitation." He challenged Griffin and Goldsberry's true motives, saying, "I think we should just call this sham of Goldsberry and Griffin about doing this for scientific sake for what it is. If we have to do scientific research, why don't we have a man like Mr. Newby, who is really qualified for this, do it and not let the fox guard the hen house?"

Newby, who had been part of the 1970 Penn Cove capture team, was asked to comment on the most authentic means and manner of marking whales efficiently in order to keep track of them. He believed this objective could be achieved if the hunters and the Game Department worked together.

Henning pointed out that twelve permits had been applied for, which, if there were only 100–115 whales in Puget Sound, equated to taking 15 percent of the population. He said, "The commission just cannot take a chance of issuing a number of permits like that and certainly not in the lower Sound where the whales have all been captured."

Goldsberry argued that if permits were not granted in Washington State, Canadians hunting the same "approximately 500 whales within the Washington and Canadian waters" would capture the animals, but they had no marking program.

Following comments about the need for more research by the Department of Game, Burton Lauckhart, chief of the Game Management Division, defended the department's approach to research in light of limited funds. He claimed that surveys showed there was a "good whale population along the coast of Washington and British Columbia" with "no indication that the few animals that have been taken have in any way harmed the existing population." If any of the wildlife managed by the agency were *endangered*, the Game Commission would take preventative action. Despite the pressure to refuse permits until more was known about the population, the Game Department wanted to keep a regulated program going and continue with its studies.

While accepting the importance of preserving the state's unique resource, Carl Crouse, on behalf of the commission, believed that their knowledge had increased but added a cautionary note: "We are somewhat concerned that the same pod of whales is being worked on." Nonetheless, he did not want to deny people the right to see them in "first class aquariums…when they might not see them otherwise."

Crouse recommended that, with some changes (which included raising the size limit to avoid taking whales that were too small or those that would "cause any problems in the family group"), six permits should be granted to Namu Inc. for the next year. However, permits for Peter Babich were not recommended after he indicated that any whales he caught would be transported to Canada and from there handled by associates at the Vancouver Public Aquarium.

After hearing all parties, it was decided to defer the matter until May to give the Game Department the chance to consider the permit applications and make their recommendations.

While the public meeting, arguments and discussions were underway in Seattle, SeaWorld Ohio was again preparing for its summer season with the arrival at Hopkins Airport of Shamu and a consignment of other marine mammals and animals brought in to entertain the public.[2] In true showbiz style, a monkey greeted the plane. Shamu, wearing a huge pair of yellow-rimmed sunglasses, was unloaded in a crate with the words "Shamu Goes Hollywood" emblazoned on the side. Here, the top-billing Shamu would join dolphins acting as water-skis for their trainers, sharing the limelight with visiting celebrities Debbie Reynolds and Lloyd Bridges.

At the end of the season, Shamu and companions would again be crated and loaded onto an aircraft for the flight back to SeaWorld San Diego. The only certainty was that, if they survived another year, they could expect to endure the same process all over again the following season.

Following the May meeting, the Game Commission wrote to Goldsberry on June 14, 1972, enclosing a permit to capture four killer whales. Although similar to the earlier permit granted to Namu Inc. this one included some changes and additional requirements.[3]

Namu, Incorporated, is hereby authorized to capture killer whales and remove from the wild a total of four (4). The third whale taken will be a research whale under supervision of the Department of Game and maintained by Namu, Inc. The Department will be financially obligated up to $1,500.00 for the transportation and maintenance of this whale during the period that this whale is confined. The capture and holding of these whales will be subject to the following conditions.

1. Namu, Incorporated, the above-named permittee, will deposit in escrow the sum of $3,000.00 from which $1,000.00 will be credited to the State General Fund for each whale taken under this permit.

2. Whales can be captured only in those waters of the State of Washington above a line extending from Point Wilson to Admiralty Head and those waters above the Deception Pass Bridge.

3. Whales can be captured or corralled only in nets, and there shall be no purse rings or purse lines on said nets. In addition, they can be taken where naturally or accidentally stranded with approval of the Game Department.

4. No animal shall be taken smaller than 11 feet total length, or larger than 16 feet total length.

5. The permittee must have available an adequate marine aquarium in which to condition and hold whales taken, which has been approved by

Shamu goes Hollywood, 1973, San Diego. *Wikimedia Commons.*

*the Department of Game. He shall also have the services of a competent
marine mammal veterinarian.*

*6. The Game Department, Game Management Division, in Olympia,
or the Regional Supervisor in Mount Vernon, shall be notified promptly
when any whales are being held in a net or nets, and when attempts to
capture whales are being made.*

*7. Animals contained in nets shall be surveyed and sorted promptly
under 24 hour surveillance with scuba divers on the scene. No animal
shall be confined in a net or nets for more than seven days.*

*8. Within five days after taking a killer whale, the permittee shall pay
to the Game Department the sum of $1,000.00 to be credited to the
State's General Fund as prescribed by law.*

*9. This permit is valid from the date of issuance to March 31, 1973,
in those waters authorized in section two of this permit.*

*10. The Department has the authority to take still photographs and
16mm movies of capture, branding, and other phases of marine
mammal management as they develop.*

*11. The permittee in the use of aircraft will abide by all state and
federal laws governing the same.*

12. Any whale lost during capture attempts or while confined in nets will be counted as a whale taken under the above permit.
13. The Director of Game reserves the right to cancel this permit at any time for cause or for violation of these provisions in addition to any criminal penalties prescribed by law.

A year after their first census, Mike Bigg and his research team conducted another survey on August 1–3, 1972. The results did nothing to allay their earlier fears and confirmed the low numbers previously recorded. In their second year of cruising through Johnstone Strait, Vancouver Island, Bigg and his team photographed a whale with a badly injured dorsal fin, later known as Stubbs.

The encounter with Stubbs proved to be a pivotal turning point in the study of killer whales. After photographing her distinctive dorsal fin and those of other killer whales, which often showed marks of injury, Bigg realized that if these were permanent nicks and scars, such distinguishing features could be used for identification of each whale. This was to be the start of the groundbreaking discovery that, in years to come, would lead to the documenting of not only the Southern and Northern Resident orca but also many others worldwide.

Namu Inc. and Peter Babich were not the only applicants for permits to capture killer whales in Washington State that year. On October 15, 1972, SeaWorld Inc. applied for a permit authorizing the taking, transportation and keeping of four killer whales.[4]

Meanwhile, the machinery of law was at work at the federal level. On October 25, 1972, President Richard M. Nixon signed the 1972 Marine Mammal Protection Act (MMPA). States' rights in the management of marine mammals within waters of state jurisdiction were about to be preempted by federal law.

On December 21, 1972, the MMPA came into force, prohibiting the taking of marine mammals from U.S. waters or by U.S. citizens in international waters, except by special permit. "Take" was defined as "the act of hunting, killing, capture, and/or harassment of any marine mammal, or the attempt at such."

Management of cetaceans under the MMPA was administered by National Marine Fisheries Service (NMFS), part of National Oceanic and Atmospheric Administration (NOAA) within the Department of Commerce.

Although the legislation put a lid on random captures, permits continued to be granted for the capturing of whales for display in the marine park industry. Any marine park wanting to import or capture a marine mammal must file an application with NMFS under one of the exemptions. Each application must list the number and species of animals, the capture method (which it stipulated must be "humane"), names and qualifications of persons involved in the capture or transport, and the impact any capture might have on the wild population. Any application must be published in the *Federal Register* and open for public comment for thirty days.[5]

Under the AWA, responsibility for setting the standards for handling, care, treatment and transport of animals was delegated to APHIS. That body issues regulations for the minimum standards required for keeping captive marine mammals, namely transport methods, pool size, water quality, etc. The AWA provides for inspection of marine parks and similar facilities keeping captive marine mammals using government-employed veterinarians.

One person, though, decided not to carry on capturing whales any longer. Ted Griffin, the man who once posed proudly holding the key to the city of Seattle, was tired of being vilified by an increasingly hostile public and retired from the business, leaving Goldsberry to carry on alone.

CHAPTER 10

PERMIT 22

ollowing the implementation of the MMPA in December 1972, NMFS received an application from SeaWorld Inc. early in January 1973 for an "economic hardship exemption." The application was made on the basis that SeaWorld Inc. had begun a $17 million investment in the "SeaWorld of Florida" project prior to the MMPA coming into force.[1]

The facility, due to open in November 1973, was expected to attract an estimated three million visitors. As with every other SeaWorld park, the operation was designed around the same theme that had made the other two parks so successful—the killer whale. SeaWorld asked for prompt action on its request, taking into account the long lead time required for capture, training and acclimatization of the animals and the rapidly approaching opening date of the new facility. If the facility was unable to open in November 1973, SeaWorld claimed, staffing would be cut by seven hundred and the company would incur a $10 million loss.

The application was published in the *Federal Register* (the federal government's daily newspaper) on January 24, 1973. On February 14, 1973, NMFS issued a letter of intent giving exemption to SeaWorld after concluding that economic hardship within the meaning of the MMPA and its regulations existed.

On February 27, 1973, NMFS held a public hearing to discuss issuing permits to the Seattle Marine Aquarium (Namu Inc.), which was now merging with SeaWorld, for the capture of two killer whales. The original request made by the Seattle Marine Aquarium was for the capture of eight killer whales, of which two would be retained for display in Seattle. The remaining six whales (killer whales were now selling at $70,000 each) were to be sold. Because of their concerns for the welfare of the animals and the proposal to capture for resale rather than simply for display, NMFS decided to hold a public hearing.

Shortly before the hearing, the Seattle Marine Aquarium (Namu Inc.) reduced its request for eight killer whales to two. On March 6, while the public comment period was still open, it withdrew its request with prejudice (meaning it could not be refiled).

The date coincided with NMFS issuing a letter of exemption (due to expire on October 20, 1973) to SeaWorld Inc. authorizing four permits to SeaWorld Inc. San Diego for the taking of killer whales in the waters of Mexico and Alaska, as well as in certain Washington State waters under the economic hardship provision of the MMPA. The application was granted without any public hearing being held in Washington State, in whose territorial waters the whales were to be taken.

The federal government's decision to grant SeaWorld Inc. a permit to capture four killer whales met with disapproval in Washington State. Governor Daniel J. Evans (R), who served three terms from 1965 to 1977 and was a U.S. senator from 1983 to 1989, wrote to commerce secretary Frederick Dent about the permits.[2] He expressed concern that no public hearing was held in Washington State, whereas a public hearing was held in Seattle on February 27 on the issuing of permits for two killer whales to Namu Inc. He requested the opportunity to hold a public meeting before any unilateral action was taken by Washington, D.C., and asked that the four approved permits be held in abeyance until he had received the records of the public hearing in Seattle for Namu Inc.'s application. Evans expressed a wish that in the future, public hearings would be held before any more permits were issued for the capture of marine mammals in Washington State.

Those in public office were not the only ones to voice their concern. The Seattle Audubon Society also objected strongly, writing to Evans and to the Department of Ecology to register its vigorous opposition to the capture of killer whales when the population was unknown and requesting that an environmental impact statement be demanded of SeaWorld.[3]

Senator Warren G. Magnuson (D), Washington State, whose committee had approved the Marine Mammal Bill in 1972, raised the issue of SeaWorld's permit with NOAA, which replied, "There would be no significant observable impact on the status of the stock of killer whales if the exemption were granted."[4]

In the face of growing opposition, Frank A. Powell Jr., vice-president/general manager of SeaWorld Inc. San Diego, wrote to Bob Walker, special assistant to California governor Ronald Reagan (1911–2004) about the company's recent acquisition of the Seattle Marine Aquarium and its subsidiary, Namu Inc.[5] Concern in the Seattle area was not about SeaWorld's permits for collecting eighty-two marine mammals, but its permission to take four killer whales. The whales were intended for research, public viewing and education in SeaWorld's new Florida park and were a necessity for success in the field of marine biology,

Daniel J. Evans, governor of Washington from 1965 to 1977. *Photo Washington State Archives.*

ecology, education, life support systems and high-quality exhibits that made SeaWorld number one in the marine park industry, Powell argued. He requested that Governor Reagan relate the company's position and history as a sound company to Governor Evans.

The Department of Game, which as of March 1, 1973, assumed responsibility for enforcing the MMPA, wrote to Dr. George D. Millay, president of SeaWorld Inc. San Diego, saying that the department was not so much concerned with the justification of a hardship case but rather NMFS's methods in issuing the permits without any hearings.[6]

While the arguments continued, a sixteen-foot killer whale found herself at the Seattle Marine Aquarium after stranding at Ocean City, Washington, on March 12. "No-Name" made history as the first whale to undergo X-rays to establish the extent and nature of her injuries.[7] The X-rays were taken as No-Name hung in a canvas sling suspended from a crane. The exercise was not a great success due to the whale's mass of tissue and repeated vibrations from the crane's motor, which contributed to blank or blurred negatives. No-Name also spoiled some of the negatives by exhaling a film of whale breath. Despite the difficulties, the veterinarian team was able to establish that No-Name had sustained some soft tissue damage but no broken bones. The team discovered that she had a bad tooth, which probably contributed to her low weight. Her sense of echolocation had been affected, which may have contributed to the stranding.

Two months later, No-Name had gained weight on a diet of herring and was recovering.[8] But her recovery was blighted when three cruel young boys rammed a steel rod down her blowhole, similar to the attack on Cuddles in 1973. Traumatized mentally and physically by the vindictive attack, No-Name withdrew from the attentions of an untrustworthy public, choosing instead to interact with Raindrop, a female dolphin. In October 1973, No-Name was purchased by SeaWorld San Diego and renamed Sandy.[9] In June 1975, she was transferred to SeaWorld Orlando, where she remained until her death in 1977 from a cerebral hemorrhage. It is uncertain whether she was a Southern Resident or not.

Despite legislation already in effect in Canada, the Southern Residents were not safe in Canadian waters. Working under a permit to capture eight killer whales, Bob Wright of SeaLand of the Pacific, Victoria, British Columbia, netted two members of K pod in Pedder Bay, British Columbia, on August 6, 1973. Two other whales from L pod were caught on August 21. The four whales were the first to be captured in Canadian waters since 1970 and were something of a disappointment to Bob Wright because of their size.[10]

Nootka II, a female member of K pod, had been captured before (see Chapter 5) along with the rest of K pod in Yukon Harbor, Washington, in February 1967. She had been luckier on that occasion and released. This time, she was held at Pedder Bay until SeaLand of the Pacific selected her as a potential mate for Haida (captured in October 1968). However, SeaLand's hopes were dashed when Nootka II died in May 1974 of a ruptured aorta before any successful breeding program took place. By using the tree-ring method of counting tooth layers to assess age, Mike Bigg estimated she was in her thirties.[11]

Taku (K1) a twenty-one- to twenty-three-foot male, had also been caught on at least four previous occasions and, like Ruffles (J1), was released because he was too large. This time he was to be used for research purposes by Mike Bigg. After being separated from the other three whales in the late afternoon of October 26, 1973, Taku was moved to a small enclosure to enable researchers to fit a radio tag with a special harness around the base of his dorsal fin. SeaLand veterinarian Alan Hoey drilled a hole through the dorsal and bolted the transmitting device to it. Two large triangular cuts were made in the trailing edge of the dorsal fin so that he could be identified more easily.[12] Although a local anesthetic was administered for the notching and tagging procedure and Taku did not exhibit any signs of pain during the operation, once the straps restraining him were removed, Taku swam into the adjoining capture pen and tried to remove the harness.[13]

After being fed one hundred pounds of herring and a ration of vitamins, Taku was released at 11:30 a.m. the following day. Researchers hoped to track him for a month and monitor his direction of travel, but their optimism was short-lived. After only eight and a half hours following Taku from Pedder Bay to the west side of San Juan Island, the research team lost him near Spieden Channel. They had been disappointed by the quality of the transmission, which was disrupted by a ball game broadcast from Tampa, Florida.

Taku managed to evade Bigg for the next nine months. When he was eventually sighted off southern Vancouver Island with other members of K pod, both harness and transmitter were missing.

In years to come, Taku was often seen traveling close to his mother, typical behavior in male orcas, often referred to as "mothers' boys." After the loss of Pacheena (K-17) in 1994, Taku was the only adult male in K pod, which numbered fewer than twenty whales at that time. Estimated by the Center for Whale Research on San Juan Island to have been born around 1955, Taku was probably in his early forties when he disappeared in 1997. K pod now had no adult males left.

Kandy, a female member of L pod measuring almost eighteen feet long, was held at Pedder Bay until Marineland and Game Farm in Ontario purchased her as a potential mate for Kandu. For her, too, life in captivity was short—she died of acute pneumonia less than three months after being captured.[14]

Frankie, a nineteen-and-a-half-foot male member of L pod captured with Kandy, was sold to SeaWorld. Frankie, along with two beluga whales and Sandy, which had been held at the Seattle Marine Aquarium since March 1973, were flown by transport plane from Boeing Field, Seattle, to San Diego.[15] Like Kandy, Frankie was not in captivity for long. He died of pneumonia five months after their joint capture.[16]

Nootka II, Taku, Kandy and Frankie were the last *known* Southern Residents to be captured. The *Journal of the Fisheries Research Board of Canada*[17] shows that between July 1964 and August 1973, a total of 43 whales were captured in British Columbia, 20 of which were released or escaped. Of those remaining, 22 were kept; 1 died. In Washington State, between September 1962 and March 1973, a total of 220 whales were captured, of which 181 escaped or were released. Of this group, 28 were kept; 11

died. Yet despite Mike Bigg's assessments of the number of killer whales off the coast of British Columbia, the captures continued. Further research and data compilation was needed to establish the status of killer whales in Canadian waters.

After returning to Johnstone Strait in August 1973 to conduct their third census, Mike Bigg and his team were able to confirm from the many photographs taken that some of the whales seen were familiar. During their research, they noted nicks and scratches on dorsal fins, scars on skin and varying pigmentation in the light gray of the saddle patches, the area behind the dorsal fin. Each saddle patch is different, not only in its overall appearance but also between the left and right side.

Other members of the research team in Nanaimo were closely examining thousands of photos of killer whales captured during the 1960s and early 1970s and were able to identify whales from their nicks, scratches and saddle patches. As the study developed, Bigg's dedicated research revealed a distinct pattern: some whales had been captured more than once, and younger members of the pod were removed every time.

Bigg was now able to start building up a picture of the family pods. It was the beginning of one of the most intriguing, and revealing, discoveries about the lives of wild orcas, which developed into the realization that not only were there two types of killer whale in the region, Residents and Transients, but also that the resident pods were split into two communities—the Southern Resident killer whales who mostly frequented the waters of Washington State, and the Northern Resident killer whales in British Columbia. Some years later, in August 1990, another ecotype of killer whale was discovered off Vancouver Island, Canada, known as the "Offshores."

With the growing evidence that he was seeing the same whales over and over, Bigg calculated that there were no more than 200-250 killer whales along the British Columbia coast and expressed grave concern about the effect the "cropping" was having on such a small population.[18] Sadly, his findings were not enough to bring an end to the ongoing captures, nor was the passing of the Endangered Species Act on December 28, 1973. The act provided for the conservation of species that are endangered or threatened, together with the conservation of the ecosystems on which they depend. Listing a species as endangered makes it illegal to "take" (meaning to harass, harm, pursue, trap, hunt, shoot, wound, kill, capture, collect or attempt to engage in any such conduct) a member of an endangered species. Similar prohibitions usually extend to threatened species, but under the ESA, there are no specific definitions of "harass" or "pursue."

It would be another thirty-two years before the Southern Resident killer whales were listed as endangered under the act and able to enjoy the protection they desperately needed to help them to survive.

With the letter of exemption from NMFS procured, on October 15, 1973, SeaWorld Inc. applied for a public display permit to capture a minimum of four killer whales for its new park in Florida.[19] From previous experience and on the advice of veterinarians and trainers, SeaWorld had found that it was less stressful on killer whales if the animals performed in pairs. Therefore, two teams of animals were required so that they could be alternated. The animals would be displayed from four to twelve times a day, on an alternating basis, for short periods of time, depending on the time of year and number of visitors. A trainer would present the whales to the public using the animals' normal behavioral characteristics so that they, the public, could appreciate the size, shape, adaptability, character and intelligence of the animals.

SeaWorld requested "collection" of a minimum of four whales, male or female, aged one to twelve years and ten to twenty feet in length, but no pregnant females. Timing for captures was crucial, depending on where the whales were and the availability of a capture vessel and SeaWorld crew. October 1 to the middle of June offered the best opportunity.

Although killer whale population stocks were still unknown, SeaWorld Inc. was one of the groups interested in undertaking a population study. It claimed that pods of killer whales numbering two hundred, three hundred or many more were often seen in the capture areas, with three groups of more than two hundred whales each seen by American and Canadian fishermen during the winter. Salmon fishermen had reported one group of more than three hundred whales. Although these numbers were only estimates, if they were accurate, the number of killer whales in the Pacific Northwest was in the thousands. The unconfirmed killer whale population was estimated at about ten thousand. From conversations with fishermen, it was apparent that sightings of killer whales were almost a daily occurrence. They were not an endangered species.

Being a publicly owned company with over five thousand stockholders, SeaWorld tried to make a profit every year and was able to upgrade and expand existing facilities to match the increase in visitors. The company was a leader in both innovation and displays and was able to supply informative and educational presentations of all types of marine animals.

SeaWorld had attracted over two million visitors that year, and it was estimated that over five million Americans and other visitors would be taking advantage of the educational entertainment in the three parks the following year, while learning about the ocean and ecology.

Programs being conducted at the San Diego and Ohio parks would also be implemented in the new Florida Park. The San Diego Department of Education had worked with more than 100,000 students participating in education tours, and while they were extremely successful, an even more extensive program was needed to include an education program involving classroom participation prior to visiting SeaWorld, an "in park" experience to develop thematic programs for study based on educational animal behavior shows and continuing educational program development.

Working in conjunction with the San Diego Department of Education, the Scripps Institute, the University of California, the Smithsonian Institution (where the remains of any whales would be taken) and the San Diego Naval Undersea Research and Development Center, SeaWorld offered many educational opportunities to students every year.

On February 7, 1974, SeaWorld Inc.'s application for a federal permit to capture four killer whales was heard in Seattle.[20] It is not clear whether a public hearing was held or not. The Washington State Department of Game requested that, as per the permit previously issued by the state on June 14, 1972, to Namu Inc., the southern part of Puget Sound should remain off limits.[21] Two months later, Senator Magnuson wrote to NOAA inquiring whether designation of Puget Sound as a whale sanctuary was possible under the MMPA. He also requested that Puget Sound be designated a "no capture area" and that NMFS issue no more permits, including any that might be pending. The Department of Game also wrote to NOAA requesting approval and funding for a whale count to be undertaken.[22]

SeaWorld's application for a permit was granted on May 7, 1974. SeaWorld Inc. was asked to pay $200 for the permit, which allowed it to capture four killer whales of either sex. Males were to be between eleven and eighteen feet in length, females between eleven and sixteen feet in length. The whales could be caught off Canada, Mexico, Washington or Alaska or within Washington waters, but captures in Puget Sound were prohibited from Priest Point on the eastern shore of Possession Sound to Nodule Point on the western shore of Admiralty Inlet and bounded on the south by the Tacoma Narrows Bridge. Permit 22, valid until December 31, 1976, was modified on August 23, 1974, and further modified on February 14, 1975.[23]

Little did company officials know it would be the last permit issued to them in the state of Washington.

CHAPTER 11

END OF AN ERA

In March 1976, a significant chain of events was put into motion that would ultimately end the capture of killer whales in Washington State. March 7, 1976, is a date that will be indelibly imprinted on the memories of Ralph and Karen Hanson Munro.[1] At the time, Munro was an aide to Governor Evans before becoming secretary of state from 1980 to 2001. Both he and Karen clearly recall the day they witnessed six killer whales being driven into Budd Inlet, Olympia, capital of Washington State.

The couple had arranged to go sailing with friends Bill and Pennie Oliver on Bill's thirty-three-foot sailboat *Mistral*. It was a holiday weekend, and the forecast was favorable.

The party was in good spirits as it set off in sunshine. The mood was uplifted further when, southbound after returning from Cooper Point, the friends spotted the rhythmic rising and falling of dorsal fins heading south past Gull Harbor, Budd Inlet. Bill changed course and slowed down. As *Mistral* sailed toward the whales, the party noticed two other boats, the *Pacific Maid* (owned by Peter Babich) and a powerful gill-netter. It soon became obvious from the boats' erratic movements that the whales were being chased; the boats slowed down when the whales dove, speeding up whenever they surfaced.

Bill began making calls to determine if the pursuers had permits. It was Sunday afternoon—not a good time to find anyone in authority. The Seattle Coast Guard said the matter was out of its jurisdiction and advised Bill to call the Game or Fisheries Departments.[2] They decided their best course

Ralph Munro, thirteenth secretary of state of Washington (in office 1980–2001), October 2013. *Author collection.*

of action was to continue observing the trawler and gill-netter, which had dropped an orange marker buoy over the side.

Bill tried to head off the pursuing boats and turn the whales away from the shallow areas of the bay. As *Mistral* motored down the inlet, a red-and-white seaplane came into view, landing nearby. The pilot swung open the door. The boating party asked him to radio for assistance. He told them that he was helping with the capture, which was being conducted under the required permit with the appropriate fisheries' personnel in attendance.

They continued to follow the capture boats until the whales were between them and the shore at Butler Cove. As the boats slowed and *Mistral* advanced, someone on the *Pacific Maid* shouted a warning to stay away. Bill ignored the warning and circled *Mistral* in front of the trawler into Butler Cove. The whales turned north, making a desperate bid for freedom.

The trawler and gill-netter set off again in pursuit. The sailing party watched with growing optimism as the whales, swimming as fast as their flagging energy allowed, appeared to gain distance and make headway out of the inlet. But optimism soon changed to dismay as the seaplane revved its engines. Churning the water white, it taxied around the bay, forcing the whales toward the east side of the channel and the orange buoy. Once the plane was in position, the gill-netter dropped a line of nets from west to east across the channel. The *Pacific Maid* followed, dropping more nets and effectively blocking any exit route.

The worst was yet to come. While the whales were herded toward the waiting nets, a smaller boat repeatedly zigzagged at high speed nearby. The sailing party watched in horror as two men repeatedly lit and threw explosives into the water one after the other. Munro reckoned they threw up to one hundred firecrackers (seal bombs) overboard to further confuse the terrified whales and drive them into the closing nets. The Munros will never forget the high-pitched squeals and shrieks of the disoriented pod rolling and spy-hopping in their attempts to escape from the ear-piercing noise. As Munro has said many times since, "It was gruesome, gruesome…the most gruesome thing I have ever seen." When *Mistral* and its outraged crew tried to move closer to the scene of carnage, two men on the trawler yelled at them again to stay away.

By now the whales were reaching the exhaustion point, having been chased and harangued for almost three days by a whaling party of thirty men headed by Donald Goldsberry.[3] The chase had started in Seattle on Friday after a fisherman spotted whales and tipped off Goldsberry, continuing through Tacoma Narrows and lower Puget Sound to Budd Inlet, where the whales were now trapped, unable to feed, unable to rest and unable to escape.

The result of the three-day hunt yielded six Transient killer whales (T13, T14, T26, T27, T46 and T47) captured off Athens Beach, Olympia, the first to be captured under the 1972 MMPA. The catch of six was soon reduced to five when one lucky whale slipped under the net and escaped.

Bill reluctantly sailed *Mistral* and its subdued crew back to shore. There was nothing more anyone could do.

Munro and his wife were haunted by the sheer brutality of the barbaric scene and unable to forget the screams of the terrorized whales. They decided the media was their best option and started calling the newsrooms. Every call but one went unanswered. *Seattle P-I* journalist Mike Layton, who was about to visit a sick relative, grudgingly agreed to take a look before dark.

The couple slept little that night. As they tossed and turned, each wondered whether Mike Layton would be true to his word or not.

At 4:30 a.m., Munro heard the *Seattle P-I* delivery van rumble past the house. He hurried out, scooping up the papers and peering through the early morning gloom. Instantly, he saw the bold black headlines: "Hundreds Watch at Olympia Harbor—Five Killer Whales Captured." Rushing back indoors, he shouted, "We just won round one. Mike Layton has written one hell of a good story."[4]

Layton's report confirmed that officials from the Department of Game were on the water monitoring the hunt. A game officer, watching the hunt from home, said the department's only function was to observe and "see that there are no illegal killings and that no unnecessary harm comes to the whales." The explosive devices were firecrackers used as a herding mechanism; there was no evidence that they were destructive to marine life, and their use was permissible under Goldsberry's permit. Any whale injured or killed would count as one of the four authorized under the permit—that was the safeguard. A state game official had said he was not aware of any depth charges being dropped from the plane, while marine mammal veterinarian Tag Gornall called the operation "humane."[5]

Then the media frenzy began. A reluctant Goldsberry told reporters that he was not sure whether the captured whales were within the legal limit as specified by the permit as they still had to be weighed and measured. He and his team would keep up the hunt for whales until they had obtained the number allowed under the permit, destined for SeaWorld aquariums in Orlando, Aurora and San Diego. The estimated value of each animal was between $60,000 and $100,000 or more.[6]

Slade Gorton, fourteenth attorney general of Washington (in office 1969–1981). *Photo United States Congress.*

Munro called Slade Gorton, the state's attorney general. Gorton agreed that decisive action was needed and instructed Munro to be at his office at noon. There he found five lawyers waiting for him.

With the whales still imprisoned in the nets, angry phone calls against the captures were pouring in. Goldsberry defended the use of "depth charges," saying they couldn't kill a fish, let alone hurt a whale. He maintained his affection for the whales, holding tight to the claim that he and his team had done more for killer whales than all the environmentalists put together.[7]

As tensions rose, a rolling veil of fog shrouded the capture scene, providing a welcome curtain from accusing eyes. The only sound puncturing the eerie silence was the bleak booming of the Dofflemeyer Point foghorn and the intermittent blows of the trapped whales. Press boats with eager journalists intent on a good story lurked near the capture site, shouting questions to the crew of the *Pacific Maid*. Four canoeists paddled alongside the net, despite warning blasts from the trawler's horn. They dispersed when a capture-team's boat backed its propellers close to one of them.[8]

About forty other protestors, mostly from Evergreen State College, converged on Beverley Beach with canoes and rowboats strapped on top of their cars. The students were undaunted by opposition from local residents who refused to let them park their cars or launch their boats from the private beach and moved farther north. Their resilience was rewarded when the whale that had managed to escape earlier unexpectedly joined them.[9]

Accompanied by the mournful wailing of bagpipes, protestors shouted to Goldsberry's crew, "Remember what happened to Captain Ahab."

Folksinger Mel Gregory, on board the Evergreen flagship *Gandalph*, sang a plaintive song about orcas making love on the ocean floor. Some of the protestors planned to present Goldsberry with "the First Olympia Bicentennial Bad Citizenship Award" but were too late as he had left by seaplane.

Someone else, though, was eager to speak with the press: Graham McDade, owner of a Seattle public relations agency who was earning thirty dollars an hour to speak about how SeaWorld was acting in the interests of the general public and, of course, doing the whales a favor by capturing them for marine biologists to study.[10]

More than one hundred people demonstrated along the shoreline of Puget Sound, and huge "Free the Whales" signs appeared in Olympia. About two hundred or more angry protestors gathered outside the Seattle Marine Aquarium displaying billboards reading "Free the Budd Inlet whales."

On Alaskan Way, near the Seattle Marine Aquarium, protestors slowed rush hour traffic, handing leaflets to passing motorists. About 150 people, including John Huskinson, president of the environmentalist group Friends of the Dolphins took part in a rally at the University of Washington urging protestors to get down to Olympia with boats, bathtubs and anything that would float. Another member suggested a national effort to raise enough money to buy the whales but was shouted down with the cry that the whales were not Goldsberry's to sell.

As the public outcry grew, the first whale to be weighed and measured was hoisted on board the sixty-five-foot trawler *Genius*. Disappointingly for SeaWorld, it was outside the legal limit and heading for freedom, but not before University of Washington professor Albert Erickson fitted the animal with a radio transmitter.[11] He said that tagging whales with transmitters would enable scientists to study their migration path and gain knowledge about behavior.[12]

Meanwhile, a resolution sponsored by Senator Magnuson (cited as "Conservationist of the Year")[13] was narrowly approved in the state senate, calling on Congress to declare an immediate moratorium on the intimidation, harassment, hunting and capturing of killer whales in Puget Sound and adjacent waters. Supported by Senator Henry Jackson (D), Magnuson also proposed creation of a whale sanctuary.[14]

By late Tuesday, Governor Evans and the attorney general had reached the decision to file a lawsuit. A new sense of urgency prevailed following word from Boston Harbor, just north of Olympia, about the arrival of a large truck, a warning signal that plans were afoot to move the whales.

Transient orcas captured in Budd Inlet, Olympia, in March 1976. *Photo John Huskinson, courtesy of Ralph Munro and Orca Network.*

The next morning, March 10, the state filed suit in the U.S. District Court to block the removal of the whales and determine whether the permit and the captures were in compliance with federal law. Even if the permit was in order, the question remained whether the use of explosive devices and aircraft could be considered "humane." Governor Evans, Attorney General

Whale hoisted on board *Genius* for weighing and measuring in Budd Inlet in March 1976. *Photo John Huskinson, courtesy of Ralph Munro and Orca Network.*

Slade Gorton and Thurston County resident Darrel Peeples (an attorney and private citizen) acted as plaintiffs against SeaWorld Inc., Donald Goldsberry, SeaWorld veterinarian Lanny Cornell and others.

The plaintiffs were successful. At the early evening hearing in Seattle, U.S. District judge Morell E. Sharp handed down a temporary restraining order prohibiting the whales' captors from removing them from Puget Sound. The order would remain in effect until "further order of the court." The judge put a condition on the restraining order, requiring a $3,000 bond from the plaintiffs but refused their request to release the whales saying it would cause "irreparable loss" to the defendants pending a final decision on their fate.[15]

Frustrated at the continuing delay, Goldsberry expressed his concern that a storm or low tide would necessitate his having to release the whales. They were not being fed to avoid them becoming reliant on the boats, he said, and needed empty stomachs when transported.[16]

With the judge's order in effect, Munro wasted no time in looking for a bail bondsman (a person or corporation that will act as a surety and pledge money or property as bail for the appearance of persons accused in court), no easy task at 9:30 p.m. The only person he could think of to call at home was a man named Dave Sprague. Munro recounted the conversation:

> *"Dave, this is Ralph Munro."*
> *I re-identified who I was as I wasn't sure he remembered me.*
> *"I know who you are, you were that trouble maker at Western Washington College."*
> *I started laughing on the phone and said, "Well, I need a bond."*
> *He said, "What's wrong, is someone in jail?"*
> *So I said, "No, we need a bond for four killer whales."*
> *Then he started laughing…*

The $3,000 bond was posted at 1:00 a.m. by Munro and Malachy R. Murphy, lead assistant to the attorney general. It was a cold night as, accompanied by a fisheries' officer, they motored through stormy water to serve the papers on Goldsberry. As their boat approached the capture site, a massive black-and-white shape suddenly exploded from the water, "scaring the hell out of us…" Munro recalled with a wry smile.

Knowing that the whales were guarded constantly and uncertain of their reception, the three men were wary as they drew alongside the *Pacific Maid*. Now, more than ten years after the curious young college student jostled for space on Deception Pass Bridge to catch a glimpse of Namu, Munro was about to come face-to-face with one of the whale's victorious captors.

Whatever he might have been thinking and feeling when the men boarded the trawler, Goldsberry remained cordial and invited them into the wheelhouse with the offer of coffee. They declined, explaining that they were on official business. After a brief conversation, the papers were served, and the state's representatives departed, leaving Goldsberry to contemplate the consequences of his actions to the sporadic accompaniment of the whales' blows and sour smell of their breath.

Evans returned from his skiing holiday to a storm of protest amid rumors that SeaWorld planned to renew its attempts to lift the whales from the water. Determined environmentalists discussed creating a boat blockade if the court gave permission to move the animals, and representatives from British Columbia–based Greenpeace and Friends of the Dolphins boarded the *Pacific Maid* to raise concerns about the feeding and care of the whales.[17] As if to cheer them on, the whale that had escaped from the net earlier in the week swam close by.

SeaWorld representative Polly Rash confirmed that the plans would proceed, providing the weather cooperated, while conceding that the temporary restraining order might prevent such activity.[18] She vociferously defended SeaWorld's actions, claiming that it was just a small group of dissidents that was trying to get its own way. SeaWorld had never before encountered such opposition, said Rash, who had begun to wonder whether it was safe to walk down the street wearing a SeaWorld jacket.[19] In nearby Beverly Beach, residents complained about SeaWorld representatives using a private dock.

While controversy raged, SeaWorld veterinarian Lanny Cornell worried about worsening weather conditions threatening the safety of the whales. He defended the company's position, saying that more whales were needed for "companionship" for those whales already held at SeaWorld parks.[20] Meanwhile, the capture and confinement operation was costing SeaWorld $5,000 a day.

Tempers flared further when people learned that the president of SeaWorld Inc., David DeMott, had visited Point Defiance Park in Tacoma in the past month and expressed interest in leasing part of the six-hundred-acre site as a possible replacement for the Seattle Marine Aquarium.[21] His timing could not have been worse.

By late Friday, March 12, the sweet taste of victory for the environmentalists and freedom for the whales was in sight. After reconvening on the fourth floor of the federal courthouse under the direction of Judge Morell Sharp, shortly after 4:00 p.m., the judge ordered that the whales be released, as their lives were in danger. The judge stated it was likely that the permit had been invalidly issued and improperly executed and ordered that the secretary of commerce be made a defendant in the case. Two federal marshals were directed to carry out the release order.[22]

The judge also referred to a Department of Game agent, Dennis Ohide, who had monitored the capture as "a lowly employee of the state who had absolutely no instructions on the matter." Ohide testified that although seal control devices were used to herd the whales, he saw no inhumane use of the devices constituting a violation of the permit and said that the use of explosives was an accepted method of rounding up whales. Under cross-examination by Malachy Murphy, he admitted he had not read SeaWorld's application for a permit nor did he recall whether he had actually read the permit itself. Judge Sharp said Ohide had no training and was out on the water without instructions, which made it difficult for him to come up with any standard of humaneness.[23] At the hearing on March 22, the defendants would be required to show why the permit should not be modified or revoked.

The anxiously waiting public applauded and cheered the news. Unfortunately, their joy was short-lived. Almost before the courthouse had emptied, SeaWorld attorneys hurried to the ninth floor to seek a stay from Ninth Circuit Court judge Eugene A. Wright.[24]

An hour and a half later, SeaWorld emerged triumphant. It had succeeded in obtaining the stay, allowing it to keep the whales in captivity. Judge Wright did not grant the request to move the whales to San Juan Island but agreed they could be moved to a safer place within the jurisdiction of the court.

Ironically, while the whales' future was being thrashed out in court, the First International Orca Symposium made its debut at Evergreen State College, not far from where the whales were held. Speakers on the first day included symposium coordinator Mark Overland, Dr. Michael Tillman (NMFS), consulting northwest marine mammal veterinarian Tag Gornall, singer Mel Gregory and "whale photographer" Ken Balcomb. Marine mammalogist Dr. Terrell Newby was also scheduled to speak.[25]

On the second day of the symposium, the list of speakers included Paul Spong from the Pacific Killer Whale Foundation in British Columbia, a scientist turned orca advocate following his close interaction with Skana at the Vancouver Aquarium, and researcher and author Erich Hoyt. Goldsberry was also scheduled to speak but had a more pressing engagement—moving whales.

But by the end of the day, there were fewer whales to move. During an attempt to maneuver them onto slings, Goldsberry suffered another setback when two captives broke through the nets and escaped.[26] He was down to three whales.

Author and researcher Erich Hoyt. *Courtesy Erich Hoyt.*

A week in politics is a long time, and it had been a long one for the whales, too, which had now been in captivity for seven days.

While Judge Sharp met in chambers with attorneys from both sides on Sunday, March 14, Goldsberry successfully hoisted a nineteen-and-a-half-foot-long male (outside the legal limit of the permit) onto the *Genius* for the sixty-mile journey to the Seattle Marine Aquarium. Freedom of a kind was in the air for this whale, later named Pender, who was first destined for a research project with the University of Washington.[27]

A reception committee awaited the whale's arrival, with Friends of the Dolphins threatening to obtain an injunction preventing the university from attaching a radio transmitter to the whale. The dolphin group's spokesman, John Huskinson, accused the university of cruelty as holes would be drilled through the whale's dorsal fin in order to fit the transmitter. Dr. Douglas Chapman from the College of Fisheries said that as the dorsal fin was largely nerveless, the procedure was painless and no different than shoeing a horse. He defended the taking of killer whales in Puget Sound, claiming that it was of no importance in the big picture as there were "several thousand on the west coast of North America alone."

Now only two whales remained in the capture pen awaiting a decision on their future. With a gag order in place, attorneys met in chambers on Monday, March 15, before Judge Eugene Wright to discuss setting up a three-judge panel of the appellate court to decide whether Judge Sharp's release order should be obeyed.[28]

One whale would not be affected by any legal decision and was released "because it was too big and nobody wanted it," according to the Department of Game.[29]

That left only Pender's companion, later named Flores. She was just outside the permit's legal limit at seventeen feet, eleven and a half inches (the minimum for a female was no less than eleven feet and no greater than sixteen feet). Soon she, too, was hoisted from the waters of Budd Inlet and transported to the Seattle Marine Aquarium to join Pender, her probable son. SeaWorld had lost another Shamu.

Pender (O4), later to become T14 (the name was given to him by the British Columbia Killer Whale Adoption Program), and Flores (O5), later to become T13 (named by the same program), waited at the Seattle Marine Aquarium while Dr. Albert Erickson's researchers designed radio packs to keep track of the whales following their release. The packs would be fitted on the leading edge of each whale's dorsal fin using five stainless-steel surgical pins, four millimeters in diameter. Using minimal corrosion-resistant bolts, each pin would be bored through the fin and fall off in about a year. The VHF radio tags, each weighing around 3.0 pounds, 4.8 ounces (1.5 kilograms) were designed to transmit for several months and be received up to eighteen miles from an aircraft or five nautical miles from a boat.[30]

With criticism and controversy damaging its coveted public image, SeaWorld's San Diego–based operation defended attacks by conservationists about the use of killer whales for entertainment purposes. Executive Vice-president George Becker told the press that the company's mistake (if indeed it had made one) had been in not coming out earlier to explain its position. He maintained SeaWorld's stance that the capture had been made in compliance with the law, the whales' safety being of primary concern.[31]

Smiling public relations staff members from SeaWorld, oozing charm and easily recognizable by their smart blue blazers and beige slacks, wooed the press with offers of free trips for themselves and their families to SeaWorld.[32] Press releases were handed out to reporters titled "SeaWorld Trainers Condition Close Relationship with Killer Whales" and "SeaWorld Research Helps Humans and Whales."[33]

One member of SeaWorld's training staff, Dave Butcher, claimed that the whales were mentally healthier in a captive environment where they had no day-to-day stresses like those in the wild.[34] They never went without food, so there was no reason for them to seek freedom. Mr. Butcher described crowd-pleasing stunts such as jumping in the air as "behaviors" that the whales enjoyed performing, much as athletes would. As far as he was concerned, there was no issue with conditioning whales to perform before a crowd.

Erickson added his own comments to the highly charged scenario. He believed that capture was important for the well being of the animals, which, if left alone in the wild, could be vulnerable to pollutants. He thought it was important to learn more about their habits through research, and they were not an endangered species.

As the court hearing drew near, attorneys worked around the clock preparing their cases. One of those grilled about evidence the evening before by the attorney general's office was expert witness Terrell Newby. Another was John Crowe, the diver who had maneuvered Lolita onto the stretcher in Penn Cove and assisted in sinking the carcasses of the four calves. Their evidence was to prove crucial in bringing to an end the capture era in Washington State.

Attorneys for the prosecution and defense appeared before Judge Sharp at the Seattle Courthouse on March 22. In much the same way as he will never forget the part he played in the 1970 Penn Cove capture, Newby recalled the role he played on that day, too. He was involved in a dirty game and was given a sharp reminder of that on his way into the courthouse. According to him, as he walked down the hallway, he was approached by one of SeaWorld's top management personnel and told that if he knew what was good for him, he would keep his mouth shut or risk getting hurt.[35]

Newby did not keep his mouth shut. The whales should be given to Erickson only on the understanding that they be released quickly, he told the judge. He added that no more permits should be granted in Washington because not enough was known about the whales.

As the legal wrangling continued, the ghost of Penn Cove reasserted itself in the form of diver John Crowe's damning evidence. Adverse publicity about the death of the four young whales was not something SeaWorld welcomed in the face of an already severely tarnished image.

On the afternoon of March 23, after two weeks of demonstrations, arguments and courtroom drama, the attorney general's office and SeaWorld attorneys reached a settlement.[36] The Stipulation of Dismissal declared:

1. *This suit is dismissed with prejudice and without costs.*
2. *Two* <u>Orcinus</u> <u>Orca</u> *in the possession of Sea World, Inc. will be delivered to Dr. A. W. Erickson of the University of Washington for holding under his permit for a period of time not to exceed sixty (60) days from today.*
3. *The* <u>Orcinus</u> <u>Orca</u> *presently at Pier 56 will not be included within the four (4)* <u>Orcinus</u> <u>Orca</u> *which may be collected by Sea World under Permit 22. However, Sea World will not exercise its right under Permit 22 or successor permits to take any Killer Whales within the waters of the State of Washington.*

A week later, the U.S. Senate voted verbally to protect killer whales in Puget Sound, Washington, from being penned for public display.[37] Commerce Committee chairman Warren G. Magnuson brought the bill to the floor following the controversial capture. Reported out of committee on March 24, the measure narrowed an exemption in the MMPA allowing killer whales to be taken only for scientific research. That law allowed the Department of Commerce to issue permits for capturing marine mammals for public display as well. Before passing the bill, the Senate accepted Magnuson's amendment to specify that scientific research permitted on killer whales must be conducted without removing them from the water.

Almost a month after she was captured in Budd Inlet, on April 5, Flores was moved to a private cove at Kanaka Bay on the west side of San Juan Island, where she would stay for two weeks' study. Soon Pender would join her, and the pair would be released with radio-tracking devices.[38]

Monday, April 26: Freedom! Seven weeks after their joint capture, Pender and Flores were tagged and marked prior to release and fitted with radio-tracking devices. Erickson likened fitting the transmitters to piercing a woman's ears.[39]

Despite their ordeal, the whales did not leave immediately. After the net was pulled aside, they circled the area for a few minutes before heading in a northwesterly direction toward Canada, away from Washington State. Their departure heralded the end of an era of more than a decade of violent captures and the near total decimation of the Southern Resident killer whales. It is impossible not to ruminate on how much longer the captures might have continued and how much more irreversible damage there would have been had justice not prevailed.

For the next ten days, the whales were tracked almost continuously by boat until their signals were lost to radio interference. The data that was obtained (transmitters had a range of up to 25 miles) showed the two whales

Flores and Pender radio tagged prior to release in April 1976. *Photo Ken Balcomb, Center for Whale Research.*

Pender's permanently scarred dorsal fin. *David Ellifrit, Center for Whale Research.*

traveled at an average speed of 2.8 knots (3.22 miles per hour) and averaged 68 nautical miles (or 78 miles) a day. Occasionally, they swam as fast as 16 knots (18.4 miles per hours) but did not sustain that speed for long. Three or four short dives showed that the whales breathed for an average of twenty-one seconds. The longer dives averaged 5.77 minutes, with the longest dive being recorded at 17 minutes.[40]

Over the next five months, radio signals were picked up occasionally until the whales disappeared. When they were encountered three years later, the radio packs were gone. Where the surgical pins once were, scar tissue had built up on both whales' dorsal fins, Flores being the worst afflicted.

Pender and Flores were often sighted together around southern Vancouver Island, as well as one reported sighting in southeastern Alaska. The last sighting of Flores was in 1998; Pender, born around 1964 and, like Taku (K1), recognizable by the indentations on his dorsal fin, was last sighted in 2011, making him a good age for a Transient killer whale.

Munro still laughs about a phone call he received in Arizona early in 2001 while walking back to the hotel with John McCain, shortly after McCain left the presidential race. The call was from Chris Dunagan, a reporter from the *Bremerton Sun* who has followed the whales for years. Munro asked him, "What the hell do you want? I'm not in public office any longer." Dunagan told him that Pender was in Hood Canal on the Kitsap Peninsula, Washington State, feasting on seals. Shaking his head, Munro laughed. "I just couldn't believe it. I felt so good about that."

Of the other whales captured, T26 (born in 1966 and recognizable by a nick at the top of her fin) has been seen by David Ellifrit, a senior staff member at the Center for Whale Research, traveling with the T10s. T26 has also been seen off Victoria, British Columbia, with her daughter, T26A, again traveling with the T10s. T46 has also been sighted.

When the Whale Museum on San Juan Island started its Orca Adoption Program in 1984, the first whale to be named was Ralph (J6). Estimated as being born around 1956, Ralph did not return with J pod to the Salish Sea after the winter of 1998. On August 23, 1999, Ralph and Karen Munro were spotted at Lime Kiln State Park (also known as Whale Watch Park), on the west side of San Juan Island, which Munro, in his role as secretary of state, was instrumental in helping create. He delivered a eulogy for J6, and in the words of Susan Berta of Orca Network:[41]

It was a beautiful day in the San Juans. The sun eluding us all summer shone brightly. The whales, who hadn't been around for a few days, were traveling north up the west side of San Juan Island, arriving at the Lime Kiln Lighthouse precisely at 1:30 p.m., just as Washington Secretary of State Ralph Munro began his "Goodbye to Ralph (J6)" speech.

Incredibly, as Ralph began his talk, he was interrupted and upstaged by an amazing show of support from J6's family (but I don't think he minded…)! All three pods went frolicking by, with no less than SIX full

Karen Hanson Munro, a volunteer at Lime Kiln Interpretive Center on San Juan Island. *Photo Erin Corra.*

J6 "Ralph" & Friends sculpture by Richard Brown exhibited at Langley Whale Center on Whidbey Island. *Courtesy of Ralph Munro and Orca Network.*

Ken Balcomb at work photo-identifying Southern Residents. *Photo Erin Corra.*

breaches exploding right behind Ralph as he spoke of his strong connection with the whales, and J6 in particular, and what a great loss it is to us all to lose J6 and the other whales that did not return this year. Ralph's connection with the whales was clearly obvious to everyone there, who witnessed that magical moment that was just too perfect and precise to be a mere coincidence. Magic, maybe—but not coincidence.

After Munro finished his speech, he and Karen threw a wreath into the water to honor the passing of J6 and all the other whales lost that year—a particularly bad year, like so many before it, for losses among the Southern Resident community.

In the same year as the final curtain fell on the captures in Washington, Ken Balcomb, the "whale photographer," slipped quietly and unwittingly toward the spotlight, soon to become another key player in the continuing saga of the Southern Resident killer whales.

CHAPTER 12

THE AFTERMATH

The Center for Whale Research, under the direction of biologist Kenneth C. Balcomb III, stands on the west side of San Juan Island, Washington State, just north of Lime Kiln State Park and Lighthouse. The modest split-level property displaying a colorful mural of an orca mother and calf on the front deck overlooks Haro Strait, facing toward Vancouver Island and the jagged snowcapped peaks of the Olympic Mountains. Behind the building's unpretentious façade lie the records of years of intensive research, resulting in thousands of meticulously catalogued photographs of the Southern Resident killer whales.

Balcomb is well qualified to conduct such research.[1] After he graduated from the University of California in 1963 with a bachelor's degree in zoology, Balcomb served his apprenticeship washing dishes on the *MV Lynann*, a whale-catching boat operating out of San Francisco Bay, before obtaining employment with the U.S. Department of Interior, Bureau of Commercial Fisheries, Marine Mammal Laboratory. He collected specimens and data for the National Marine Mammal Laboratory in Seattle before moving on in 1966 to work as a field biologist for the U.S. National Museum's Pacific Ocean Biological Survey Program, where he studied and banded seabirds in the central North Pacific. During that time, Balcomb took the first photos ever of living Fraser's dolphins and made the first known observations of living Longman's beaked whales.

Between 1967 and 1972, Balcomb worked for the U.S. Navy as an oceanographic specialist and aviator tracking whales by using the SOSUS

Right: Kenneth C. Balcomb III, Center for Whale Research. *Photo by Howard Garrett.*

Below: Members of J and K pods under the watchful eye of the Center for Whale Research, San Juan Island. *David Ellifrit, Center for Whale Research.*

(Sound Surveillance System), a network of deep underwater listening posts. He took a year's break from the navy in 1972 and enrolled in a PhD program in marine biology with renowned marine-mammal biologist Dr. Ken Norris at the University of California–Santa Cruz. Although Balcomb completed the coursework, he did not spend the requisite year paying in tuition afterward, or petition for candidacy. Years later, he published his thesis studies in marine mammal science on Baird's beaked whales but has yet to return to UC to receive his PhD and says he is now too busy. After doing some work at whaling stations in Nova Scotia and Newfoundland for the Fisheries Research Board of Canada, Balcomb completed two years of active duty in Japan with the U.S. Navy.

Following Mike Bigg's recommendation in 1976 that no more killer whales be captured in Canadian waters other than to replace any that died in Canadian aquariums, Balcomb was asked by the U.S. National Marine Fisheries Service to undertake a census of killer whales in Washington State. At about the same time, he was offered the position of chief scientist on the three-mast wood barquentine *Regina Maris*. Dr. George Nichols, a diving physiology doctor and scientist from Boston, had approached Balcomb the previous year asking him to consider letting his navy commitment expire. If he did so, Nichols would purchase the *Regina Maris* for the worldwide research that Balcomb wanted to conduct. Balcomb jumped at the golden opportunity, and Nichols was true to his word. For several winters, Balcomb sailed on the *Regina Maris* photo-identifying and recording humpback whales in the North Atlantic, while studying killer whales in Washington State during the summer.

On April 1, 1976 (April Fool's Day), less than a month after the Budd Inlet saga, Balcomb began his "Orca Survey" research from Bainbridge Island, Washington State, before moving to San Juan Island in May to continue the study. His first "encounter" (the term officially used by the Center for Whale Research when in proximity to whales) was six days later, when he came across a pod of orcas and began taking the first of the fourteen thousand identification photos that would be snapped that year. It soon emerged that many of these whales had been the victims of previous captures. Like Bigg before him, it was not long before Balcomb's studies and photo-identification catalogue supported Bigg's findings that there were far fewer killer whales than originally thought. The total numbered only seventy-one.

Although enjoying the best of both worlds, researching humpback and killer whales, Balcomb still wanted to pursue his dream of building a whale museum, filled with factual information and the specimens he had collected for over a decade. In 1978, as president of the Moclips Cetalogical Society (an organization dedicated to benign methods of whale research), Balcomb rented the Odd Fellows Hall at Friday Harbor, San Juan Island, from Lee Bave for seventy-five dollars a month.

Built in 1892 by members of the Mount Dallas Lodge #95 of the Independent Order of Odd Fellows (IOOF) and originally known as the Odd Fellows Hall, the building, listed on the Washington State Heritage Register, was used to host meetings and community events. It also has a

ORCA SURVEY

THE ORCA SURVEY Is an intensive study of KILLER WHALES In the Pacific Northwest waters. Biologists aboard the 'Ballena Pacifico' In conjunction with the National Marine Fisheries Service are photographing Orcas and following the movements of recognizable individuals and or groups.

The study is purely scientific. Detailed examinations of photographs will enable researchers to identify distinctive individuals. Information gathered will give a clearer understanding of the natural biology, social behavior, and population dynamics of these animals.

PUBLIC COOPERATION is vital to the success of the study. Researchers aboard the study vessel are prepared to respond instantly to sighting calls anywhere in Washington waters.

HAVE YOU SEEN ANY KILLER WHALES?

IF YOU SEE KILLER WHALES PLEASE CALL IN YOUR SIGHTING IMMEDIATELY.

National Marine **442-4737**
Fisheries Service   collect or direct
24 hrs.

If you live on the water and wish to participate in the "Whale Spotter Information Network" please contact

Orca Survey Coordination Center
445 Wood Ave. SW
Bainbridge Island Wa. 98110
842-7558

Thank you for your cooperation. We will acknowledge your help.

Moclips Cetological Society 6/76

Orca Survey logo, 1976. *Photo by Ken Balcomb, Center for Whale Research.*

The Whale Museum, Friday Harbor, San Juan Island. *Author collection.*

darker history, having been used as a courtroom for some of the county's more notorious trials.

Balcomb's first exhibit at the Whale Museum was the skull of an orca that he obtained from Taiji when he was stationed in Japan. While driving past the docks, Balcomb noticed the orca's carcass. He shouted at the taxi driver to stop, but the request fell short due to the language barrier. Desperate to secure the prize, Balcomb jumped from the moving vehicle. His timing was perfect, as he was able to avail himself of the services of a passing English-speaking researcher from the local aquarium, who translated his request for the skull. He still had to barter for the teeth, which the fishermen planned to sell off as tuna lures at $20 each. In the end, Balcomb paid $500 for the skull, weighing 300 pounds, which he then transferred in the trunk of the cab, still covered in bloody tissue, to the local aquarium. After leaving the skull in a tidal pool for nature to do its work, he retrieved it a year later, 140 pounds lighter, and had it shipped back home under the heading of "household goods." It now rests cushioned by a sheepskin base on a small table in Balcomb's living quarters at the Center for Whale Research.[2]

In 1982, having realized his ambition and laid the foundations of what is now an internationally famous museum, Balcomb left the Whale Museum to concentrate on the photo-identification studies of the Southern Resident killer whales. He went on to found the Center for Whale Research, a nonprofit organization under "friendly" directorship, of which he has been the executive director and principal investigator since 1985. He is also a charter member of the Society for Marine Mammals, a member of the IUCN/SSC (International Union for Conservation of Nature/Species Survival Commission) and an invited specialist on the Scientific Committee of the International Whaling Commission.

The center works on a tight budget, with a mixture of regular staff members and volunteers. In the early days, Balcomb could be found selling T-shirts and buttons to help raise funds to support his research.

David Ellifrit, curator of the extensive photographic library, joined Balcomb as a staff member in 1990. His interest in whales was piqued after watching the film *Namu: My Best Friend* (a reissue of the film originally known as *Namu, the Killer Whale*). In 1984, he went up to Vancouver Island, Canada, to see Namu's mother and family, the Northern Residents. When he returned to Columbia, Missouri, David set about studying whales and soon proved his worth with his photographic and identification skills.

Identification charts of Southern Resident orcas at the Center for Whale Research. *Author collection.*

11 EASY STEPS TO PRODUCE AN ID SHOT

STEP ONE TAKE ID SHOTS ON BOAT WHEN THE WHALES ARE PERPENDICULAR TO THE BOAT. TRY TO CONCENTRATE ON ONE ANIMAL WITH DORSAL + SADDLE PATCH THE CENTER OF THE FRAME. WAIT UNTIL THE BOAT IS CLOSE ENOUGH FOR CLEAR SHOTS.

STEP TWO ON RETURN HOME FILL OUT FILMLOG WITH INFO ABOUT EACH ROLL SHOT THAT DAY. FOR EACH ROLL SHOT THE PROGRESS OF PROCESS + ANALYSIS MUST BE CHECKED BY YOU OR A STAFF MEMBER.

STEP THREE LABEL PLASTIC FILM CANISTER WITH BLANK LABELS IN BOX PROVIDED. LABEL WITH PHOTOGRAPHER'S NAME, ROLL #, DATE + POD.

STEP FOUR ALL FILM SHOULD BE PUT IN DEVELOPING ROOM, WHEN ALL FILM IS COLLECTED FROM THE DAY THEN BEGIN THE FILM DEVELOPING PROCESS (SEE DEVELOPING INSTRUCTIONS).

STEP FIVE AFTER FILM IS DRY, LABEL A CLEAR, PLASTIC NEGATIVE SHEET WITH PRINTED LABELS PROVIDED.

STEP SIX CUT YOUR FILM IN STRIPS OF 6 FRAMES BEGINNING WITH THE FIRST FRAME, PLACE IN NUMBERED ORDER IN NEGATIVE SHEET.

STEP SEVEN OBTAIN ID SHEET + WRITE YOUR NAME AT THE TOP. BEGIN IDENTIFYING WHALES IN EACH FRAME LISTING THESE ON THE 'ID SHEET.

STEP EIGHT FOR INDIVIDUAL IDENTIFICATION BEGIN WITH YOUR CLEAREST, CLOSEST SHOTS, REFERRING DIRECTLY TO THE 1988 + 1989 EARTHWATCH ORCA SURVEY CATALOGS + THE GENEOLOGY PRESENTATIONS PROVIDED. LOOK FOR SHAPE + NICKS ON DORSALS AND SCRATCHES, SCARS + SHAPE OF SADDLE PATCHES. THESE ALL IDENTIFY INDIVIDUAL WHALES. BE CAUTIOUS WITH NON-PERPENDICULAR SHOTS.

STEP NINE WHEN IDENTIFICATION OF WHALES IS COMPLETE HAVE A STAFF MEMBER CHECK YOUR FILM OVER + BEGIN COMPUTER ENTRIES OF EACH ROLL SHOT (SEE COMPUTER INSTRUCTIONS).

STEP TEN PLACE ID SHEET ALONG WITH THE NEGATIVE SHEET IN THE LABELLED ID NEGATIVE BINDER.

STEP ELEVEN AFTER QUALITY ID PHOTOGRAPHS HAVE BEEN CHOOSEN THE PRINTING PROCESS CAN BEGIN (SEE PRINTING INSTRUCTIONS).

Instructions on how to photograph a whale, provided by the Center for Whale Research. *Author collection.*

Field biologist Erin Heydenreich is also a senior staff researcher with Orca Survey and has been with the center since 2003.

Dr. Astrid van Ginneken, another long-term researcher who lives most of the year in Rotterdam, where she works as an assistant professor with the Faculty of Medicine at Erasmus University, has spent a couple of months every summer at the center since 1987. For many years, Astrid visited Gudrun, an Icelandic whale captured in October 1976 and kept at the Dolphinarium Harderwijk, Holland. Gudrun had been part of an experiment in two-way communication to see if she could learn, and use, new words. When Astrid sang Mozart arias, Gudrun responded with her own calls. After Gudrun was transferred to SeaWorld Orlando in November 1987 as part of a breeding program, Astrid continued to visit her. Sadly, Gudrun died on February 25, 1996, four days after going into labor with her third calf, which she was unable to deliver.

Stefan Jacobs, another accomplished photographer, first came to the center as an Earthwatch volunteer in 1992 and, like Astrid, returns every summer.

Despite Balcomb's ongoing studies confirming how few whales remained after the decimation of their numbers during the capture era, the path to protection for the Southern Residents was far from smooth. When a number of environmental groups petitioned NMFS in May 2001 to list the Southern Resident killer whales as "Endangered," NMFS decided to grant them protection under the MMPA on June 25, 2002, rather than list them under the Endangered Species Act. On December 18, 2002, five environmental groups and a number of individuals brought a federal action challenging NMFS's decision.[3]

Five months later, on May 29, 2003, NMFS declared the orcas "Depleted" under the MMPA. On December 17, 2003, a U.S. District Court judge instructed NMFS to reconsider their listing decision.

In a further twist, on April 3, 2004, all orcas in Washington waters were listed as "Endangered" by the State Department of Fish and Wildlife. On December 16, 2004, NMFS announced plans to list the orcas as "Threatened."

Finally, having found them to be a distinct population segment of orcas in danger of extinction, on November 18, 2005, NMFS declared the Southern Resident killer whales as "Endangered." One reason for the decision, NMFS said, was that "the capture of killer whales for public display during the 1970s likely depressed their population size and altered the population characteristics sufficiently to severely affect their reproduction and persistence."[4]

The only living member of the Southern Residents not covered by the new status was Lolita. A clause had been included in the ESA listing that excluded all captives or their progeny.

The ruling has not stopped people such as Howard Garrett of Orca Network from campaigning for Lolita's release. Experts such as Balcomb (who assisted with the captive orca Keiko's release from Mexico and his rehabilitation back to the wild) have offered their knowledge and expertise to aid and support a similar program for Lolita. The sea pen at Kanaka Bay where Pender and Flores were held in 1976 is an ideal location for her possible rehabilitation. She is a known member of L pod and responds to their calls, as was proved when a recording of L pod calls made by *Dateline NBC* was played at the Miami Seaquarium in 1996. Her family spends much of the summer around the San Juan Islands, and the west side of San Juan Island is a favored foraging and socializing area. Ocean Sun (L25), estimated as being born in 1928 and possibly Lolita's mother, is still alive.

Further up the shore from Kanaka Bay stands Lime Kiln State Park. The thirty-six-acre park was created in 1983 when the Moclips Cetalogical Society took over the lease of Lime Kiln Point Lighthouse.[5]

Like the Center for Whale Research, the park overlooks Haro Strait. The historic building is used by a number of researchers as a shore-based research laboratory for behavioral and acoustic studies on orcas, Dall's porpoise and minke whales. When the lighthouse is open, whale sightings are chalked up

L pod whales, including Lolita's possible mother, Ocean Sun (L25). *David Ellifrit, Center for Whale Research.*

Lime Kiln Lighthouse, Lime Kiln State Park, San Juan Island. *Photo Richard Snowberger.*

on a board for the benefit of visitors. The most common question asked by the public is, "What time do the whales go by?"

On July 2, 2011, enthusiastic whale watchers and dedicated volunteers from the Center for Whale Research and Orca Network gathered at Lime Kiln State Park, San Juan Island, to celebrate and commemorate a special event—the 100th birthday of Granny (J2), the oldest matriarch (and oldest member) of the Southern Resident community. The atmosphere was festive as families set out picnics under the warmth of the sun, their feet tapping to the background music of the Kevin Carr Family Band. Children sporting "fin" hats learned about whales from exhibits brought along by Jeff Hogan of Killer Whale Tales. With a wry smile, the guest speaker, Balcomb, said he hoped not to be upstaged by the whales.

Where were the whales? That was the question on everyone's lips as all eyes scanned the horizon. Earlier in the day, a telltale cluster of whale-watch boats revealed the presence of part of J pod. During June, J pod had split in two for several days, traveling as much as twenty miles apart before joining up again at the end of the month—then splitting again. The strategy is used to find food. In bygone days, when salmon was plentiful, the pod had no need to disperse in search of their essential energy bars.

Whale watchers at Lime Kiln State Park celebrating Granny's (J2) centenary. *Author collection.*

In his tribute to Granny, a whale that has survived incredible odds, Balcomb reminded his audience of the importance of bringing back the salmon. No salmon, no whales.

As Balcomb finished speaking and looked toward the sea, shining black dorsal fins glinted amid the whitecaps. Excited whale watchers surged forward to find the best vantage point along the rocky shoreline as the approaching whales dipped and dived. Cindy Hansen, educator at the Whale Museum, set up a speaker for the hydrophone, a device used to listen to the whales communicating underwater. Soon J pod's unique calls could be heard as they passed the lighthouse, fountains of mist from their powerful exhalations reflected against the glare from the sun's rays. A hush came over the assembled crowd, overawed at the magnificent spectacle of nature in the wild. David Ellifrit reeled off identifications as though reciting times tables—he didn't even carry binoculars.

As the whales passed in front of the lighthouse, whale watchers cheered in unison as one of the whales catapulted through the air in a perfect, curving arc. Two more sky-reaching breaches followed, culminating in a cloud of frothing white water as J pod paid tribute to the matriarch on her special day. One of the breaching whales was Mike (J26), named after researcher Mike

Lea (K14) shows the underside of her tail flukes. *David Ellifrit, Center for Whale Research.*

Bigg, who contributed so much to our knowledge of killer whale society before he, like so many of the Southern Resident community, died far too young on October 18, 1990.

Although Granny missed her party, she appeared bright and early the next morning not too far from the Center for Whale Research. Her probable son Ruffles (J1) was not at her side. The last sighting of this much-beloved whale was off Victoria, British Columbia, in November 2010.

So what does the future hold for the Southern Residents? They have survived persecution and cruelty beyond measure at the hands of the human race and continue to face the existing challenges of pollution from toxins, shortage of salmon and increasing vessel noise. One would like to think that their long and troubled journey to protection under the ESA is the means to their future survival. They are the most studied whales in the world, with a host of researchers and scientists working to gather information on the complex factors that threaten them.

Although the budget has been cut drastically, Balcomb's photo-identification work remains an important ongoing part of the study. Orca Network's mantra "Connecting Whales and People in the Pacific Northwest" depends on citizen science to report whale sightings and help gather data

The legendary Granny (J2), oldest member of the Southern Resident clan, breaches skyward. *David Ellifrit, Center for Whale Research.*

Ruffles (J1) born (est.) 1951 and probable mother Granny (J2) born (est.) 1911. *Photo David Ellifrit, Center for Whale Research.*

NOAA research team prepares to tag a Southern Resident orca in Admiralty Inlet.
Author collection.

about locations and movement trends. NOAA put a lot of time, money and effort into tracking the whales by ship; satellite tags deployed by crossbow or pneumatic rifles are attached to the dorsal fins to discover where they travel in the winter after leaving the inland waters of the Salish Sea. It is hoped that this somewhat controversial method will provide more answers about their feeding patterns and critical habitat.

Lightweight biopsy darts fired by pneumatic rifle are aimed at the saddle patch to collect skin and blubber samples for DNA testing. D-tag suction tags are attached to the whales using a long pole to monitor sound exposure and behavior. Tucker, a black Labrador from Conservation Canines, spends time with University of Washington researchers following the whales. He stands at the bow of the boat sniffing the air for whale scat, which is collected and taken to the laboratory for analysis. The Whale Museum's Soundwatch boat can be seen frequently on the water educating boaters about the whale watch guidelines and federal regulations to protect the orcas. Occasionally, photogrammetry (aerial photography) is used to obtain length and width measurements and can be helpful in evaluating long-term growth trends.

But let us not be lulled into a false sense of security by the sophisticated tools of research. Recently, a new threat loomed over the Southern Residents

Conservation canine Tucker sniffing for whale scat from the bow of Moja. *Author collection.*

Farmers Blimp (formerly the airship *Eureka*) hovers over the Southern Resident orcas during a photogrammetry exercise. *Author collection.*

under the sinister heading of "delisting." Two California mega-farm owners petitioned NOAA in August 2012 to review the Southern Residents' listing under the ESA. Agribusiness wanted river water for irrigation that is currently off limits because it is needed for salmon—the food of the Southern Residents. The Pacific Legal Foundation, representing the agricultural industry, claimed that the Southern Residents were no different from other orca around the world, which are not endangered. At the end of NOAA's comment period, January 28, 2013, more than 136,000 comments *against* delisting had been filed. On August 2, 2013, NOAA announced its rejection of the delisting petition, saying, "Our determination that the Southern Resident killer whale population constitutes a distinct population segment under the Endangered Species Act and previous conclusion that the distinct population segment is in danger of extinction and should remain endangered status all support our finding that the petitioned action to delist the Southern Resident killer whales distinct population segment is not warranted."[6]

But an even more insidious discovery threatens to affect the future of this beleaguered population. It is called "inbreeding." A study by researchers, including Dr. Michael J. Ford, the principle person involved in the genetic work on the Southern Resident killer whales, stated, "In particular (J1) was inferred to be the father of 8 individuals (5 from J pod)."[7]

K pod, the smallest pod, has produced mostly male calves. L pod, too, is male dominated. The tragic death of Sooke (L112) in February 2012 is a devastating blow to L pod, as she was only the second female born to the pod since 2003. Around the time of her death, Canadian military vessels were monitored on VTS (vessel traffic service) in the Salish Sea, and the use of both sonar and explosives was heard on the Lime Kiln hydrophone. It is

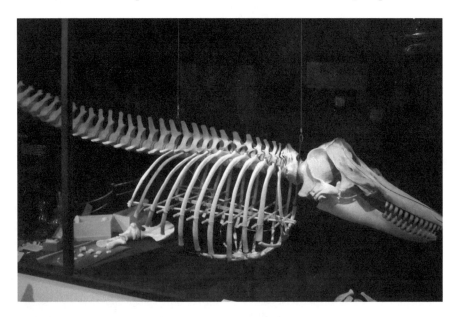

Skeleton of Sooke (L112) at the Whale Museum, Friday Harbor, San Juan Island. *Author collection.*

uncertain whether Sooke was in the area when the exercises took place. On February 25, 2014, NOAA announced its findings of the investigation into her death and concluded "blunt force trauma was the primary consideration for the acute death of the animal."[8] Although the mystery of her death may never be solved, she will not be forgotten. Her skeleton will stay with the Whale Museum. Whatever the future may bring, her story, and that of her clan, will live on through the excellent educational displays and interpretive exhibits at this popular museum in Friday Harbor.

Nobody likes a sad ending. It is heartening that Astrid van Ginneken's July 2011 study into the various factors prohibiting growth in the Southern Resident community, such as boat effects, reproductive capacity, paternity and the effects of the capture era, led her to the conclusion that, as other studies have stated that the viability of a mammal population is as low as sixty animals (as of April 2014, there are eighty Southern Residents), there is hope that the Southern Residents can still recover.[9] However, Balcomb adds the cautionary words "if Chinook salmon recover." The prognosis by salmon experts a few years ago was that all species of salmon in the region would be negatively affected by climate change (less water and warmer water in rivers of the Pacific Northwest due to global warming). If that proves to be the case, the Southern Resident orcas may shift farther north in their constant quest for food. Only time will tell.

EPILOGUE

This book began with the story of captivity, and that is where it should end, though on a somewhat different note. To quote singer Bob Dylan, "The times they are a-changin'…"

In July 2012, New York investigative journalist and author David Kirby was on San Juan Island for the signing of his book, *Death at SeaWorld: Shamu and the Dark Side of Killer Whales in Captivity*.[1] It is a harrowing tale about the brutal death of Dawn Brancheau in February 2010 following an attack by the captive whale Tilikum at SeaWorld Orlando and reveals the shocking truth about the tortured lives of captive whales. While nowadays many whales are born in captivity rather than taken from the wild, they continue to live dysfunctional lives at the hands of the corporate body that chooses to disperse and dispose of them at will. Whales are separated from family members or from other whales they may have bonded with; bullied in small, enclosed tanks from which there is no escape; and moved from one facility to another, all in the name of "entertainment."

Gabriela Cowperthwaite was also on San Juan Island in July 2012. She was directing the film *Blackfish*, which premiered at the Temple Theater in Park City, Utah, on January 19, 2013.[2] The film, one of forty-three independent films selected for the Sundance Film Festival from over two thousand, is another exposé of Dawn's tragic death and Tilikum's sad life. Four days into the festival, the film was snapped up by CNN Films, a production and acquisition unit of CNN Worldwide, and the Wagner/Cuban Companies' Magnolia pictures. *Blackfish* has received rave reviews and has drawn

The tragedy of Tilikum, dorsal fin collapsed, head downwards symbolizing death; the faces honor those that lost their lives. *Courtesy artist Kelli Clifton.*

international acclaim, including nomination for the British Academy Film and Television Awards, the equivalent of the Oscars.

New Zealand orca researcher/advocate Dr. Ingrid Visser has not been afraid to speak out against captivity, hitting the headlines with her fight to free Morgan, a young orca rescued in Holland and now on public display at Loro Parque in Tenerife, Spain.

Two men still living with their memories of a bygone era are Ted Griffin and Donald Goldsberry. Neither welcomes the attentions of the press. After he finished capturing whales in 1972, Griffin went into seclusion in eastern Washington. John Stone remembers him coming into the Captain Whidbey Inn some years later. When Stone said, "You're Ted Griffin," he denied it, saying he was a rancher. According to a report in the *South Florida Sun-Sentinel* in 2004, he has not changed his opinions with the passage of time.[3]

In May 2010, investigative journalist Tim Zimmermann, who writes for *Outside Magazine*, obtained a rare interview with Goldsberry at his home near Sea-Tac Airport.[4] Now in his late seventies, Goldsberry is not in the best of health and has an oxygen tube clipped to his nose. Sipping on a mug of vodka and ice, he, like Griffin, shows no signs of regret. After being run out of Washington State, he carried on catching whales in Iceland to supply marine parks, including SeaWorld. One of those whales was Tilikum.

Both men have enjoyed the fruits of success. At one time, Griffin owned a waterfront home on Bainbridge Island and an island in the San Juans; Goldsberry had homes in the Bahamas and on San Juan Island, where the whales pass by. His boat, *Killer Whale*, was often moored in Friday Harbor.

Until July 2012, a shabby trawler listlessly rode the gentle wash from the many boats entering and leaving Friday Harbor. Tourists making their way to the waiting whale-watch boats barely glanced at the *Genius*, one of ten purse-seiners constructed at the Skansie Shipyard in Gig Harbor. Once one of the best-known tenders packing fish in Puget Sound, its shady past as one of the purse-seiners involved in the last capture of whales in Washington State will soon be buried a little deeper in history as the Crosby family undertake renovations and restore its pride.[5]

The Stipulation of Dismissal saw the light of day again in 2002 when a two-year-old orphaned calf, Springer (A73), a member of the A5 Northern Resident pod, strayed into Puget Sound, Washington State, alone and ailing. A few months earlier, in a strange twist of fate, a young Southern Resident male, Luna, (L98), was discovered alone in Nootka Sound, British Columbia, having become separated from his pod. The big question of what was best for both Luna and Springer had to be resolved. Various marine parks offered to assist with Springer's "long term rehabilitation." After Ralph Munro retrieved the Stipulation of Dismissal, a timely reminder was given that SeaWorld was not welcome in Washington State.

With the U.S. and Canadian governments, citizens and environmental organizations working together, Springer was successfully reintegrated with her pod. Veterinarian Dr. Pete Schroeder, who accompanied the original Shamu to San Diego, contributed his expertise to the project and oversaw Springer's release, an accomplishment of which he is justifiably proud. In July 2012, several events were scheduled in British Columbia and Washington State to celebrate Springer's ten years with her family. Now there is even greater cause to celebrate Springer's life in the wild with her family—she was seen swimming with a calf of her own near Bella Bella, British Columbia, on July 4, 2013.

Tsu'xiit ✳ Luna ✳ L98

September 19, 1999 – March 10, 2006

Tsu'xiit was born near the San Juan Islands on September 19, 1999, and was found alone in Nootka Sound in July 2001, three days after the passing of Mowachaht/Muchalaht Tyee Ha'wilth Ambrose Maquinna.

Maquinna had told Ha'wilth Jerry Jack that he would return as a kakawin (killer whale). Luna's arrival was seen as a spiritual reflection of his deep love for his people, community and hahoulthee (traditional territory). Luna was named "Tsu'xiit" in his honour.

The controversy surrounding Luna's presence in Nootka Sound peaked in the summer of 2004 when the Department of Fisheries and Oceans were confronted by Mowachaht/Muchalaht canoes, determined to keep Tsu'xiit free. Tsu'xiit was recognized as the return of Ha'wilth Ambrose Maquinna consistent with the cultural beliefs of the Mowachaht/Muchalaht First Nations.

"Since time immemorial we've stood by each and every animal and living thing within our territory. For the past few years, we've been honoured by the presence of the whale. We have a lot to be proud of as Mowachaht/Muchalaht people, for upholding our beliefs of letting nature take its course, and keeping Tsu'xiit free". Chief Michael Maquinna.

For 18 months, various Stewards watched over Luna as the controversy continued. Then, on March 10, 2006 it all ended. The young whale was killed instantly after being pulled into the prop of the General Jackson, a 30 meter tug pulling a fully loaded log barge.

The name "Luna" was heard around the world. He touched a lot of lives and brought a community together; united with strong cultural and historical ties with the kakawin.

Above: *Genius* in Friday Harbor, San Juan Island (July 2012). *Author collection.*

Right: In memory of Luna (L98), Gold River, Nootka Sound, Vancouver Island, British Columbia. *Photo Richard Snowberger.*

Above, left: Dr. Terrell Newby speaking on board *MV Indigo* at the 2010 Penn Cove capture commemoration. *Author collection.*

Above, right: A reflective Wallie Funk at Coupeville Wharf for the 2010 Penn Cove capture commemoration. *Author collection.*

Vern Olsen sings "Lolita Come Home" at the annual Penn Cove commemoration. *Author collection.*

Luna's poignant tale has a different ending and is told in two beautifully documented films, *Saving Luna* and *The Whale*, produced and directed by Michael Parfit and Suzanne Chisholm of Mountainside Films Ltd, and their book, *The Lost Whale*.

How will Lolita's story end? The only surviving Southern Resident still in captivity today may yet receive a reprieve from the prison she has endured with amazing fortitude since 1970. In response to a request from a number of petitioners to include Lolita in the ESA listing of the Southern Resident killer whales, on January 24, 2014, NOAA Fisheries announced a "12-month finding and proposed rule to revise the endangered listing of the Southern Resident killer whale distinct population segment to include Lolita." Along with the many people waiting to hear the outcome are former diver John Crowe, who lives in Oregon, and Terrell Newby, who works as a volunteer at the Veterans Hospital in Seattle. On his office wall is a picture of the Penn Cove capture. The graphic photo of the whales corralled in the nets serves to remind Newby of a different era, when whales were for sale at $20,000 each and marine parks from across the globe waited to take them. He candidly admits that the screams of the whales and his memories of the capture have always bothered him.

Passengers on board the Washington State ferry enjoy a rare treat as Southern Residents head out of Admiralty Inlet past Whidbey Island. *Author collection.*

Susan Berta and Howard Garrett, of the Orca Network, at the opening of the Langley Whale Center, Whidbey Island, March 2014. *Photo Mary Jo Adams.*

John Crowe makes a heartfelt plea for Lolita's return. *Photo courtesy of* News-Times, *Newport, Oregon.*

One thing is for certain—Lolita will never be forgotten in Washington State. Every year, on or around August 8, Howard Garrett and Susan Berta of Orca Network hold a commemoration to honor the whales captured and killed in Penn Cove and as a living memorial to Lolita. Captain John Colby Stone's fifty-two-foot ketch *Cutty Sark* leads a flotilla of smaller boats and kayaks to the 1970 and 1971 capture sites. On the fortieth commemoration of Lolita's capture, Ralph and Karen Munro, Terrell Newby and Wallie Funk were present. As an evergreen wreath and roses were strewn across the waters that once ran with blood, Vern Olsen reached for his piano accordion and sang the song he wrote for Lolita, "Lolita Come Home."

In the summer of 2014, Washington State Ferries will launch a new ferry. Thanks largely to the efforts of Susan Berta and Howard Garrett, the ferry will be named *Tokitae* to honor the little whale taken from her home waters so long ago. If justice comes full circle, the real Tokitae may yet swim alongside her namesake in Puget Sound.

NOTES

Chapter 1

1. Puget Sound, http://en.wikipedia.org/wiki/Puget_Sound.
2. Admiralty Inlet, http://en.wikipedia.org/wiki/Admiralty_Inlet.
3. Deception Pass, http://en.wikipedia.org/wiki/Deception_Pass.
4. http://www.nmfs.noaa.gov/pr/species/mammals/cetaceans/killerwhale.htm.
5. http://orcanetwork.org/nathist/nathist.html.

Chapter 2

1. *Miami News*, "Six Men Capture a Killer Whale," November 19, 1961.
2. *Quebec Chronicle-Telegraph*, "Killer Whale Taken From Harbor," November 20, 1961.
3. *St. Joseph (MO) Gazette*, "Captured Killer Whale Dies," November 21, 1961.
4. http://cetacousin.bplaced.net/captive/orca/profile/Wanda.html.
5. "A Whale of a Business," PBS's *Frontline*, http://www.pbs.org/wgbh/pages/frontline/shows/whales/etc.cron.html.
6. George W. Klontz, M.S., D.V.M., "Medical Care of Newly Captured Killer Whales," *Southwestern Veterinarian Journal*, summer 1970.
7. Moby Doll Symposium, May 2013, Saturna Island, British Columbia.
8. *Vancouver (BC) Sun*, "Two Battle Killer Whale in Strait," July 16, 1974.
9. Terry Hammond, "Wounded Whale Swims in on Leash," *Vancouver (BC) Sun*, July 17, 1964.

10. "A Whale of a Business," PBS's *Frontline*, http://www.pbs.org/wgbh/pages/frontline/shows/whales/etc/orcas1.html.
11. *Montreal Gazette*, "Killer Whale on Display in Harbor," July 20, 1964.
12. *Dubuque (IA) Telegraph Herald*, "Female Killer Whale Heads for New Home," July 23, 1964.
13. https//circle.ubc.ca/bitstream/handle/2429/30498/ubc_2011_spring_werner_mark.pdf?sequence=6.
14. *Montreal Gazette*, "Looks Healthy but Killer Whale Still Spurns Food," August 6, 1964.
15. *Eugene (OR) Bulletin*, "Killer Whale Moby Doll Dies Friday," October 10, 1964.
16. Jacques-Yves Cousteau and Philippe Diole, *The Undersea Discoveries of Jacques-Yves Cousteau: The Whale* (New York: Arrowood Press, 1987).
17. http://www.pbs.org/wgbh/pages/frontline/shows/whales/etc/orcas1.html.

Chapter 3

1. "A Whale of a Business," PBS's *Frontline*, interview with Ted Griffin, www.pbs.org/wgbh/pages/frontline/shows/whales/interviews/griffin.html.
2. *Miami News*, "Fisherman Nets 2 Killer Whales," June 25, 1965
3. *Montreal Gazette*, "'Killer' Bought for $8,000," June 29, 1965.
4. Ted Griffin, *Namu—Quest for the Killer Whale* (Seattle, WA: Gryphon West Publishers, 1982).
5. *SI Vault*, "For a Killer Whale Caught in a Cage," http://sportsillustrated.cnn.com/vault/article/magazine/MAG1077463/3/index.htm.
6. "Shamu, Shamu…The Dark History Behind the Chant," http://withoutmethereisnou.wordpress.com/2011/04/05.
7. *Montreal Gazette*, "Heat Troubles Whale Namu, but He Eats," August 3, 1965.
8. *Regina (SK) Leader-Post*, "Killer Whale Is Big Money-Maker," September 20, 1965.
9. *Reading (PA) Reading-Eagle*, "Killer Whale Put Owner in Debt," August 20, 1966.

Chapter 4

1. Griffin, *Namu*.
2. *Seattle P-I*, Extracted notes November 2, 1965 and November 5, 1965.
3. *Richland (WA) Tri-City Herald*, "San Diego Park Buys Killer Whale," December 13, 1965.
4. *Modesto (CA) Bee*, "Watch that Whale, George—She's a Killer," San Diego (AP), December 21, 1965.
5. *Oxnard (CA) Press Courier*, Jack McQuarrie, "San Diego's Sea World, a Major Southland Attraction—A World of Sea Magic," February 9, 1969.
6. *Sarasota (FL) Herald Tribune*, "Killer Whale Rescued in Ohio," May 4, 1971.
7. http:law.justia.com/cases/California/calapp3d/64/1.html–Eckis v SeaWorld Corp. 64 Cal.App.3d.1.
8. Erich Hoyt, *Orca: The Whale Called Killer*, Appendix 6, "Killer Whales Kept Captive" (Camden East, Ontario: Camden House Publishing, 1990 ed.).

Chapter 5

1. *Spokane (WA) Spokesman Review*, "Cow Whale Escapes from Net," January 10, 1966.
2. *Reading (PA) Eagle*, "Killer Whales Are Captured in Northwest," February 16, 1967.
3. Hoyt, *Orca*, Appendix 5, "Live-Capture Statistics for Killer Whales."
4. George W. Klontz, M.S., D.V.M., "Medical Care of Newly Captured Killer Whales," *Southwestern Veterinarian Journal*, summer 1970.
5. *Vancouver (BC) Sun*, "Walter Comes to Aquarium and It's a Whale of a Sale," March 20, 1967.
6. *Saskatoon (SK) Star-Phoenix*, "Whale of a Time Awaits Walter," March 11, 1967.
7. *Vancouver (BC) Sun*, "Walter Is Really Whale of a Girl," March 21, 1967.
8. *St. Joseph (MO) News-Press*, "Killer Whales 'Talk' Over Telephone," March 17, 1967.
9. *Vancouver (BC) Sun*, "Is Our Whale Expecting?" May 9, 1967.
10. Hoyt, *Orca*, 143.
11. *Miami News*, "A Whale's Try to Save a Dolphin," March 21, 1969.
12. *Spokane (WA) Daily Chronicle*, "Famed Whale Succumbs," October 6, 1980.
13. "Whale of a Business," PBS *Frontline*, Interview with John Hall. http://www.pbs.org/wgbh/pages/frontline/shows/whales/man/ramu.html.

14. *Pittsburgh (PA) Post Gazette,* "Can Killer Whales Find Happiness?" March 14, 1967.

15. *Lodi (CA) News Sentinel,* photograph of Chester the chimp with his head in Kilroy's mouth, October 19, 1968.

16. George W. Klontz, M.S., D.V.M., "Medical Care of Newly Captured Killer Whales," *Southwestern Veterinarian Journal* (summer 1970).

17. *Spokane (WA) Spokesman-Review,* "Whale aided by Firemen," December 4, 1967.

18. Cathy Neville, "Neck with a Whale for Big Kiss," *Spokane Daily Chronicle,* June 13, 1968.

19. *Oxnard (CA) Press Courier,* "Sea World Buys Killer Whale," December 4, 1969.

20. http://cetacousin.bplaced.net/orca/profile/kandu.html.

21. *Jeannette (PA) News-Dispatch,* photo of Lupa being lowered into New York City Aquarium's "Polar Bay," April 8, 1968.

22. *Milwaukee (WI) Journal,* "InDentured Service: Brushing During Meals Solves Problem at Aquarium," June 14, 1968.

23. Stefan Jacobs, http://www.orcahome.de/incidents.htm.

24. *Eugene (OR) Register-Guard,* "NY Whale Dies in Pool," September 7, 1968.

25. *Boca Raton (FL) News,* "Lolita: Happy, Gentle, Smart; Weighs 4 Tons," December 2, 1981.

26. http://www.freewebs.com/let_toki_go_free/hugotheorca.htm.

27. Norton Mockridge, "Hugo Stars in a Whale of an Act," *Toledo (WA) Blade,* February 1, 1971.

28. *Rome News-Tribune,* "Hugo the Killer," July 25, 1971.

29. *St. Petersburg (FL) Times,* "Little Olga Meets 'Hugo' the Killer Whale," March 19, 1973.

30. *Daytona (FL) Morning Journal,* "Killer Whale Hugo Dies," March 4, 1980.

31. http://www.orcanetwork.org/captivity/lolitacapture.html.

32. Hoyt, *Orca,* Appendix 5 and 6.

33. Clark A. Bowers, et al., Naval Undersea Center, San Diego, California, Ref. Article Ref. AD-754 396, "Project Deep Ops: Deep Object Recovery with Pilot and Killer Whales," distributed by National Technical Information Service, U.S. Department of Commerce, 5285 Port Royal Road, Springfield, VA, 2215.

34. *Vancouver Sun,* "Young Killer Whale Arrives as Star of Marine Show," April 15, 1969.

35. *Ellensburg (WA) Daily Record,* "Killer Whale Blues Piped Away," November 21, 1971.

36. *Ottawa Citizen*, "Probe Urged into Whale's Death," October 4, 1982.
37. *Vancouver Sun*, "Bacteria Led to Death of Killer Whale Haida, Examination Revealed," October 5, 1982.
38. Alexandra Morton, *Listening to Whales* (New York: Ballantine Books, 2002), 149.
39. *Nashua (NH) Telegraph*, November 26, 1968.
40. *Windsor (ON) Star*, "A Whale of a Job," January 27, 1969.
41. E-mail from Doug Cartlidge, former trainer, June 2, 2011.
42. "Cuddles," http://www.britishpathe.com/video/cuddles-the-killer-whale.
43. *Bryan (OH) Times*, "Whale Escaped Injury," January 20, 1973.
44. *Pittsburgh (PA) Press*, "Zoo Trying to Sell Whale," December 14, 1973.
45. *Glasgow (Scotland, UK) Evening Times*, "Zoo's Killer Whale Cuddles Is Dead," February 7, 1974.
46. *Melbourne (Australia) Age*, "Whale Gets Jet Ride to Surfers," March 11, 1970.
47. *Montreal Gazette*, "Ulcers Lay Low Ramu the Whale," May 18, 1970.

Chapter 6

1. *Whidbey (WA) News-Times*, Eric Nalder, "Whale Deaths May Help Legislation," November 26, 1970.
2. "Notes on the Natural History of the Killer Whale *Orcinus orca* in Washington State," *Murrelet* 53, no. 2 (May–August 1972): 22–24.
3. *Port Townsend (WA) Leader*, "The Great Whale Hunt," January 29, 1970.
4. Hoyt, *Orca*, Appendix 5.
5. *Seattle Times*, "Killer Whales Stage 'Salt-Water Ballet,'" August 9, 1970.
6. Ibid., "Killer Whales Captured Off Whidbey Island," August 8, 1970.
7. *Seattle P-I*, "Dozens of Killer Whales Caged at Whidbey," August 9, 1970.
8. Comments by Captain John Colby Stone at the Penn Cove Commemoration, August 7, 2011.
9. *Everett (WA) Herald*, "Whidbey Whale Capture Said Reason for Law," August 10, 1970.
10. Ibid., "Regulate Whale Captures," August 25, 1970.
11. Personal interview with Dr. Terrell Newby, July 26, 2011.
12. *Everett (WA) Herald*, "Whidbey Whale Watch Grows Bigger on Island," August 11, 1970.

13. *Whidbey (WA) News-Times*, "Appeal for Whale Brings Fed Reply," September 3, 1970.
14. Ibid., "Killer Whale Meets Fans on Ferry Ride to Seattle," August 13, 1970.
15. *Seattle P-I*, "Whale Power Comes Down on Aquarium," August 23, 1970.
16. Comments by Pixie Maylor at the Penn Cove Commemoration, August 7, 2011.
17. Val Varney, "Whales Draw Spectators to Aquarium," clipping from unknown newspaper, August 16, 1970.
18. *Seattle Times*, "'Lot of People Concerned,' 50 Pickets Protest Treatment of Whales," August 23, 1970.
19. Mary Syreen, "Whale Turns Up on Beach and on Public Mind," *Whidbey (WA) News-Times*, September 24, 1970.
20. *Whidbey (WA) News-Times*, "Two More Whales Wash Up on Beach," November 12, 1970.
21. Claudia D. Hansen, "Islanders Find Another Dead Whale," *Everett (WA) Herald*, November 20, 1970.
22. *Seattle Times*, "Hunter 'Checking Into' Whale Deaths," November 23, 1970.
23. Claudia D. Hansen, "Anchor Number Main Clue in Hunt for Whale Killers," *Everett (WA) Herald*, undated copy.
24. *South Whidbey (WA) Record*, "Penn Cove Orca Round Up Recalled," http://www.southwhidbeyrecord.com/news/20428949.html.
25. E-mail communication from Dr. Terrell Newby, April 10, 2013.

Chapter 7

1. Copy of untitled newspaper clipping (date stamped August 19, 1970).
2. http://cetacousin.bplaced.net/orca/profile/chappy.html.
3. http://cetacousin.bplaced.net/orca/profile/jumbo.html.
4. http://cetacousin.bplaced.net/orca/profile/clovis.html.
5. http://cetacousin.bplaced.net/orca/profile/winston.html.
6. Wayne Reid, "RAMU: A report on Inter-species Relationships and the Transport of a Large Marine Mammal," http://aquaticmammalsjournal.org/share/AquaticMammalsIssueArchives/1977/Aquatic_Mammals_5_2/Reid.pdf.
7. E-mail from Doug Cartlidge, June 2, 2011.
8. http://freegreekdolphins.blogspot.com/2011/04/dolphins-in-attica-sunday-times-march.html.

9. Vanessa Williams, "Captive Orcas 'Dying to Entertain You'—the Full Story," report for Whale and Dolphin Conservation Society, Chippenham, UK, April 30, 2001, www.wdcs.org/submissions_bin/orcareport.pdf.

10. Dr. Susan Brown and Dr. Margaret Klinowska review of marine parks, www.marineanimalwelfare.com/review.htm.

11. "Winnie's Page," http://www.angelfire.com/gu/orcas/winnie.html.

12. *Eugene (OR) Bulletin*, "Killer Whale Flown by Jet to Australia," October 8, 1970.

13. http://www.orcanetwork.org/captivity/lolitacapture.html.

14. http://miamiseaprison.com/tank.htm.

15. *Bainbridge (WA) Review*, "How to Catch a Whale," August 12, 1970.

16. *Pittsburgh (PA) Press*, "Performing Whale Dies in Germany," October 6, 1971.

17. *Seattle Times*, "Import of Whale Products Banned," November 24, 1970.

18. Eric Nalder, "Whale Research Center Threatened with Move," *Whidbey (WA) News-Times*, November 5, 1970.

Chapter 8

1. Copy of undated newspaper clipping (date stamp February 28, 1971) relating to law passed regulating future captures.

2. Notes among Washington State Archives.

3. Killer whale permit dated August 20, 1971, issued by Department of Game, Washington State, copy supplied by United States Department of Commerce, National Oceanic and Atmospheric Administration, National Marine Fisheries Service under FOIA.

4. Garry Garrison, Game Management Supervisor, Game Management Division, Washington State Department of Game, "Killer Whale Management," Washington State Archives.

5. Michael Bigg, Summary, July 26, 1971, killer whale census, Fisheries Research Board of Canada, Biological Station, Nanaimo, British Columbia.

6. *Whidbey (WA) News-Times*, "So Do the Hunters—Whales Return," August 26, 1971.

7. Hoyt, *Orca*, Appendix 5.

8. Don McGaffin's memoir supplied by Mimi Sheridan.

9. "Branding of Killer Whale on August 27, 1971," Washington State Archives.

10. *Windsor (ON) Star*, "Coffee, Tea or Milk, Mr. Dick?" November 1, 1971.

11. "Libby Davies, MP," http://en.wikipedia.org/wiki/MarineLand.
12. *Eugene (OR) Register-Guard*, "Shamu Dies of Infection," August 31, 1971.
13. http://cetacousin.bplaced.net/orca/profile/seq714.html.
14. E-mail from Graeme Ellis (August 01, 2012), Pacific Biological Station, Department of Fisheries and Oceans, Nanaimo, British Columbia.
15. http://cetacousin.bplaced.net/orca/profile/canuck.html.
16. Garry Garrison, Game Management Supervisor, Game Management Division, Washington State Department of Game "Killer Whale Management," Washington State Archives.

Chapter 9

1. Notes of Public Hearing, Capture of Killer Whales, State Game Commission Meeting, April 11, 1972, Washington State Archives.
2. "Remembering Sea World of Ohio in the 70s," http://newsnet5.com/dpp/news/local_news/remembering-sea-world-of-ohio-in-the-70s.
3. Letter from Department of Game to Donald Goldsberry, June 14, 1972, and Killer Whale Permit issued by Department of Game, Washington, copies supplied by United States Department of Commerce, National Oceanic and Atmospheric Administration, National Marine Fisheries Service under FOIA.
4. United States District Court of the Western District of Washington at Seattle, Amended Complaint No. C7657T, item 19 relating to Sea World's application on October 15, 1972, Washington State Archives.
5. http://www.pbs.org/wgbh/pages/frontline/shows/whales/etc/laws.html.

Chapter 10

1. Letter from Frederick B. Dent, secretary of commerce, Washington, D.C., to the Honorable Daniel J. Evans, date stamped April 3, 1973, Washington State Archives.
2. Letter from the Honorable Daniel J. Evans to the Honorable Frederick B. Dent, March 9, 1973, Washington State Archives.
3. Letter from Seattle Audubon Society to Governor Daniel J. Evans, March 12, 1973, Washington State Archives.
4. Included in memo "to Governor from Elliot," March 12, 1976, Washington State Archives.

5. Letter from Frank A. Powell Jr., vice-president/general manager of SeaWorld Inc., to Mr. Bob Walker, special assistant to the governor, Sacramento, March 20, 1973, Washington State Archives.
6. Letter from Department of Game to Mr. George D. Millay, president, SeaWorld Inc., March 20, 1973, Washington State Archives.
7. *Spokane (WA) Spokesman Review*, "Killer Whale X-rayed," March 22, 1973.
8. *Richland (WA) Tri-City Herald*, "No-Name Finds Unlikely Friend," June 1, 1973.
9. "Sandy," http://cetacousin.bplaced.net/orca/profile/sandy.html.
10. *Vancouver Sun*, "Researchers to Get Captured Whales," August 31, 1973.
11. Hoyt, *Orca*, 123–24.
12. Ibid., 123.
13. The Whale Museum, Friday Harbor, San Juan Island, Washington State.
14. http://cetacousin.bplaced.net/orca/profile/kandy.html.
15. *Lodi (CA) News-Sentinel*, "Whales to Ride Guppy," October 25, 1973.
16. *Montreal Gazette*, "Pneumonia Killed Killer Whale," November 21, 1973.
17. *Journal of the Fisheries Research Board of Canada* 7 (July 1976).
18. Hoyt, *Orca*, 69.
19. SeaWorld: Application for Public Display Permit under the Marine Mammal Protection Act of 1972, October 15, 1973, Washington State Archives.
20. Included in memo "to Governor from Elliot," March 12, 1976, Washington State Archives.
21. Ibid.
22. Ibid.
23. Permit 22 dated May 7, 1974, issued by U.S. Department of Commerce, National Oceanic and Atmospheric Administration, NMFS (Permit to Take Marine Mammals), modifications dated August 23, 1974 and February 14, 1975, copies supplied under FOIA.

Chapter 11

1. Personal interview with Ralph Munro and Karen Hanson Munro, April 9, 2011.
2. Affidavit of William H. Oliver dated March 10, 1976, Washington State Archives.
3. *Olympia (WA) Daily Olympian*, "TRAPPED! 5 Killer Whales Netted in Budd Inlet Yesterday," March 8, 1976.

4. *Seattle P-I*, Mike Layton and Kirk Smith, "Hundreds Watch at Olympia Harbor—Five Killer Whales Captured," March 8, 1976.

5. *Anchorage (AL) Daily News*, "Whale Hunt to Continue Despite Flap," March 8, 1976.

6. *Ellensburgh (WA) Daily Record*, "Dispute Rages Over Whales," March 9, 1976.

7. *Lewiston (ID) Morning Tribune*, "Whale Capture Stirs Furor," March 9, 1976.

8. Steve Kelley, "Whale Protests Cut Fog on Budd Inlet," *Olympia (WA) Daily Olympian*, March 9, 1976.

9. *Spokane (WA) Spokesman Review*, "Protestors Find Snag on Beach," March 10, 1976.

10. Bill Cameron, "Orcas Captured in Budd Inlet," *Olympia (WA) Cooper Point Journal*, March 11, 1976.

11. *Olympia (WA) News Tribune*, "Killer Hoisted Aboard," March 15, 1976.

12. *Spokane (WA) Daily Chronicle*, "Last Whales Released," April 26, 1976.

13. *Seattle P-I*, "Magnuson Cited as 'Conservationist of Year,'" March 10, 1976.

14. *Spokane (WA) Spokesman Review*, "State Suit Seeks Whale Hunt Ban," March 11, 1976.

15. *Ellensburgh (OR) Daily Record*, "Restraining Order Will Keep Whales Temporarily in Sound," March 11, 1976.

16. Eric Nalder and Jack Hopkins, "Transfer of 5 Whales Halted by U.S. Judge," *Seattle P-I*, March 11, 1976.

17. Paul Andrews, "Whales under 1901 Law?" *Seattle Times*, March 12, 1976.

18. *Seattle Times*, "'Hefting' of Captive Whales Planned Anew," March 11, 1976.

19. *Youngstown (OH) Vindicator*, "Whales Create Dispute," March 11, 1976.

20. *Seattle P-I*, "State's Sad Harvest Should Be Halted," March 10, 1976.

21. Kerry Webster, "Rumor Has Point Defiance as Captured Whales' Home," *Tacoma (WA) News Tribune*, March 11, 1976.

22. *Seattle P-I*, "Appeals Judge Stays Killer Whales' Release," March 13, 1976.

23. Paul Andrews, "Most Didn't Stay for 'Final' Verdict," *Seattle P-I*, March 13, 1976.

24. Don Hannula, "Appeals Judge Reverses Order," *Seattle Times*, March 13, 1976.

25. "The First International Orca Symposium Tentative Schedule, March 4, 1976," Washington State Archives.

26. *Wisconsin State Journal*, "Two Captive Whales Escape," March 15, 1976.

27. Kerry Webster, "Killer Whales Plentiful, Professor Claims," *Tacoma (WA) News Tribune,* March 15, 1976.
28. *Seattle P-I,* "Captive Whale Free," March 15, 1976
29. *Eugene (OR) Register-Guard,* "Captive Whales Happy While Disposition Argued," March 16, 1976.
30. http://www.orcahome.de/t13andt14.htm.
31. *Eugene (OR) Register-Guard,* "Sea World Objects to 'Captain Ahab' Image," March 19, 1976.
32. Personal interview with Ralph Munro.
33. *Eugene (OR) Register-Guard,* "Sea World Objects to 'Captain Ahab' Image," March 19, 1976.
34. *Lewiston (ID) Morning Tribune,* "The Great Whale War," March 19, 1976.
35. E-mail communication from Dr. Terrell Newby, April 10, 2013.
36. Copy of United States District Court Western District of Washington at Tacoma No. C-76-57T Stipulation of Dismissal dated March 23, 1976, Washington State Archives.
37. Energy and Environment article titled "Killer Whales," Washington State Archives, April 3, 1976.
38. *Spokane (WA) Spokesman-Review,* "Whale Release Still Two Weeks Off," April 6, 1976.
39. Ibid., "Scientists Don't Agree on Killer Whale Studies," March 24, 1976.
40. http://www.orcahome.de/t13andt14.htm.
41. "Orca Network Ceremony and Tradition, August 24, 1999," www.orcanetwork.org.

Chapter 12

1. Personal communication with Kenneth C. Balcomb III.
2. Center for Whale Research, http://www.whaleresearch.com.
3. Personal communication with Orca Network.
4. http://www.nmfs.noaa.gov/pr/species/mammals/cetaceans/killerwhales.htm.
5. Tracie Hornung, "The History of the Whale Museum," http://www.whale-museum.org.
6. *San Juan (WA) Journal,* "Petition to Delist Southern Resident Killer Whales Rejected," August 2, 2013, http://www.sanjuanjournal.com/news/218184042.html.

7. Dr. Michael J. Ford et al., "Inferred Paternity and Male Reproductive Success in a Killer Whale (*Orcinus orca*) Population," *Journal of Heredity Advance Access*, July 14, 2011.

8. "Final report on Sooke (L112)," http://www.westcoast.fisheries.noaa.gov/protected_species/marine_mammals/killer_whale/l112/stranding_final_report.html.

9. Lecture notes by Astrid van Ginneken, July 6, 2011.

Epilogue

1. David Kirby, *Death at Sea-World: Shamu and the Dark Side of Killer Whales in Captivity* (New York: St Martin's Press, 2012).

2. http://blackfishmovie.com.

3. "Marine Animal Capture Is a Big, Bad Business," Bahamas News Archive Top Stories. http://www.bahamasb2b.com/news/wmview.php?ArtID=3654.

4. Tim Zimmermann, interview with Donald Goldsberry, May 2010.

5. A Genius Project, http://funds.gofundme.com/Genius.

ABOUT THE AUTHOR

 andra Pollard was brought up in Cornwall, England, and now lives on Whidbey Island, Washington State. She is a certified marine naturalist giving land- and boat-based talks about the endangered Southern Resident orcas and other marine mammals of the Salish Sea; a volunteer with the local whale sightings organization, Orca Network; and a member of the Central Puget Sound Marine Mammal Stranding Network. As a freelance writer, she has written articles and short stories for various publications in both the UK and United States.

Visit us at
www.historypress.net

....

This title is also available as an e-book